A GEOGRAPHY OF GOD

Exploring the Christian Journey

Michael L. Lindvall

Westminster John Knox Press
LOUISVILLE • LONDON

Previously published as *The Christian Life: A Geography of God,* Foundations of Christian Faith (Louisville, KY: Geneva Press, 2001).

Book design by Sharon Adams
Cover design by Pam Poll Graphic Design
Cover photographer/artist: Stephen Johnson/Getty Images

First edition
Published by Westminster John Knox Press
Louisville, Kentucky

This book is printed on acid-free paper that meets the American National Standards Institute Z39.48 standard. ∞

PRINTED IN THE UNITED STATES OF AMERICA

07 08 09 10 11 12 13 14 15 16 — 10 9 8 7 6 5 4 3 2 1

Library of Congress Cataloging-in-Publication Data is on file at the Library of Congress, Washington, D.C.

ISBN-13: 978-0-664-23072-2
ISBN-10: 0-664-23072-5

Contents

Acknowledgments

Other journeys may be solitary, but no faith journey is solo. We are becoming who we are not just by the grace of God, but in the company of those who are on the road with us, through the wisdom of those who pointed out the way when we were lost, and by the mercy of those who helped us to our feet when we stumbled.

I am thankful to Westminster John Knox Press for its ongoing faith in this book and to my editor, David Maxwell, for many careful suggestions that have surely made this a better volume.

Most of all, I thank my wife, Terri, for her consistent inspiration; she walks the faith quietly, but steadfastly.

PART I   Leaving for Home

Chapter 1

Spiritual Maps

*T*he novelist John Gardner once generalized that there are only two plots to all the stories ever told: *a stranger came to town,* and *someone went on a journey.* The Christian faith includes both. The Bible is populated with a string of strangers come to town: Abraham, Jacob, Moses, most certainly Jesus, and in one place after another, Paul. And the people of Scripture are the kind of folks who don't much stay put. They travel from Ur of the Chaldees to the promised land, out of Egypt and back to that land of milk and honey, up and down the Galilee and then to Jerusalem. Finally, these travelers crisscross the known world. But it's not only the ancients who met strangers come to town and then went on journeys, both outward and inward. The One who once came as a stranger to fishermen and tax collectors comes to us now, again as a stranger. And these ages later, he still invites us to rise and go on a journey ourselves.

In my experience, few people have been argued into believing in God. Nevertheless, I have begun this book with a whiff of apologia— "apologetics" in the old sense of the word: a reasonable argument for believing in something beyond yourself. Those of us contemplating the journey, even those who are already on the road, need to remember that it is a reasonable quest after all. At the far end of this volume, I have included many pages that have about them something of a faith manual—specific, even "practical" suggestions for how you might live in faith from one day to the next. In my experience, however, there are as many ways to be a Christian as there are Christians.

This book is divided into three parts: "Leaving for Home," "The Way," and "Life on the Road." The first, in the tradition of apologia, offers a response to the obvious question, "Why go any-where at all, spiritually speaking?" The second part names what I have come to believe to be the road. This is the way found in the God that the Christian tradition has long understood (as best mere mortals might understand Divinity) by the ancient map of God called the Trinity. In the eloquent and ancient terms of Trinitarian theology, the "stranger come to town" becomes "the knowable stranger" and not quite a stranger at all. The last and largest part describes life on the road as I and other pilgrims have known it. Here are traveling companions to be met; I will introduce you to some of those who have helped me find my way. In these pages are mile-markers and road signs, warnings of perilous curves, refreshment for the weary, and notice of lovely things to be seen along the way by watchful eyes.

Some twenty years ago, the philosopher E. F. Schumacher wrote a remarkable little book called *A Guide for the Perplexed*. It is a subtle and complex argument for the Christian faith that begins with this story:

> On a visit to Leningrad some years ago I consulted a map to find out where I was, but I could not make it out. From where I stood, I could see several enormous churches, yet there was no trace of any of them on my map. When finally an interpreter came to help me, he said, "We don't show churches on our maps." Contradicting him, I pointed to one that was very clearly marked. "That is a museum," he said, "not what we call a living church. It is only the living churches that we don't show."

Schumacher then offers a personal reflection on this oddity of Soviet-era mapmaking:

> It occurred to me that this was not the first time I had been given a map which failed to show many things that I could see right in front of me. All through school and university I had been given maps of life and knowledge on which there was hardly a trace of many of the things that I most cared about and that seemed to be of the greatest possible importance to the conduct of my life.[1]

Those who would make spiritual journeys need spiritual maps. But the little book before you is not an attempt to make another one. The map, if you will, has already been drawn. I would only point it out for the benefit of those restless for the journey. I will also offer thoughts about how to read this ancient map and hints about what you might experience as you travel. In the end, the most eloquent testimony to the Christian faith is the word of those who have taken the road before us and found more than they first sought along the way.

Chapter 2

Rise and Shine

*M*y wife is an early-morning runner, so I'm seldom the first person up at our house. I'm usually second, and for some years it was my job to wake our teenage son. I had to do this because when he was fifteen and sixteen, he was more-or-less impervious to alarm clocks. Waking him up in the morning was a delicious pleasure, because for the first five years of his life he woke me up. Until he was five, the child never slept, or so it seemed. In truth, he slept in brief snatches and kept his parents awake night after night.

My wife was doubtless up with him ten hours to my one during those years. Nevertheless, my memories are still keen enough to remember musing as I sat with him at three in the morning that there would come a day in perhaps a decade when I would get to go into this kid's bedroom when he was sleeping soundly and shout, "Benjamin! Wake up!" And then I would imagine him rolling away from me, pulling the pillow over his head and saying, "No, Dad, no! Not yet! Please!" And then I would say, "Yes, now! It's four thirty in the morning, and it's time to get up." He would moan, and I would reach down and shake him by his shoulder and rouse *him* out of *his* sound sleep.

Now I do get to wake him up every morning, but, oddly enough for a teenager, he is remarkably easy to rouse. I come into his bedroom at 6:40 and say the same words that my father (or was it my mother?) said to me and my brothers: "Rise and shine!" And he does. At least he rises, and then after a long shower and a bowl of breakfast cereal he may shine.

"Rise and shine" are biblical words; they are more or less the first words of the sixtieth chapter of Isaiah. After I had heard them as a child and then quoted them to my son like a mantra, it dawned on me one early morning that these old words invite a question: Why? Why get up in the morning at all, much less "shine"? What will this day mean? What do all the days piled up on top of each other mean? What is life for?

I run the risk of tidy generalization, but I think there are basically two answers to the question. The first reason to get up in the morning is that there may well be things that will please you in the sixteen to seventeen hours to come, and anyway, you *have to*. You get up in the morning because you have to eat and because people expect things of you. Somebody's got to pay the bills and mow the lawn and take the Jeep in for an oil change. You get up because you like to play hockey, or your job is often an interesting challenge, or you look forward to an evening with friends. Sometimes when I wake Ben up in the morning, I toss one of these number-one reasons at him: "Ben, you have to be at school on time." "Benjamin, you've got a 9:20 hockey game in Pontiac; the coach called and he needs you to play left wing, and anyway, you'll have a great time."

At its bleakest, the first reason for getting up in the morning is that you simply must: the day's progression of activities that keep life chugging along, food on the table, gas in the car, and chaos at bay. At its best, this first reason for living declares that you really can enjoy life. Your job may give you satisfaction; you enjoy growing tomatoes or playing pickup hockey. Even better, you rise and shine because you find that being with people, especially people you care about, gives you great pleasure. At its best, the first reason to live is that you have been able to fill your days with some sweet things, good food, interesting events, and pleasant people, all of which more or less conspire to justify getting out of bed.

In the late 1980s, *Life* magazine ran a feature article that asked forty-nine oddly assorted Americans to pen a few words in response to the question, "What are we here for?" The writers included movie stars, cabbies, even a handful of theologians and philosophers. One Jose Martinez of New York City offered a startlingly frank summary of why he gets up in the morning: "We're here to die, just live and die. I drive a cab. I do some fishing, take my girl out, pay taxes, do a little reading, then get ready to drop dead. You've got to be strong about it."[1]

Taken together, "you gotta" and *la dolce vita* form a credible reason to rise and shine. For many people, it is all the reason for living they ever expect or experience. Perhaps they are oddly blessed, or maybe they are oddly cursed. Part of me is tempted to envy acquaintances who seem content to spend their days without feeling pulled beyond a life of obligation and personal satisfaction. Another part of me wonders if providence will ever bless them with uneasiness.

But for many of us, perhaps most of us sooner or later, a life lived for reasons no more than duty and pleasure becomes soup too thin to sustain life. This awareness grows slowly in some, like the tide rising to the legs of your beach chair while you have your nose in a book. It intrudes into other lives like a bolt of lightning out of a sudden summer thunderstorm. Either way, it demands a response to the older and deeper questions: What does life mean? Is there a God after all? And if there is, can I know anything about such mystery?

The British newspaper columnist Bernard Levin wrote an op-ed piece some years ago in which he said this:

> Countries like ours are full of people who have all the material comforts they desire, together with such non-material blessings as a happy family, and yet lead lives of quiet, and at times noisy, desperation, understanding nothing but the fact that there is a hole inside them that however much food and drink they pour into it, however many motor cars and television sets they stuff into it, however many well balanced children and loyal friends they parade around the edges of it . . . it aches.[2]

Few of his readers know that before his early death, the French existentialist novelist Albert Camus frequently attended the American Church in Paris. He even discussed the possibility of baptism with the pastor:

> The reason I have been coming to church is because I am seeking. I'm almost on a pilgrimage—seeking something to fill the void that I am experiencing—no one else knows. Certainly the public and the readers of my novels, while they see that void, are not finding the answers in what they are reading. But deep down you are right—I am searching for something that the world is not giving me.[3]

There comes the day in many lives when living for little but good pleasure, even the nobler pleasures of personal achievement and loving relationships, can no longer fill the void. The pages of your Franklin Planner unfold nowhere except into another year and then into the year after that. What the world names success cannot altogether satisfy the hunger—not the career, not the great house, not the one-in-a-million apartment, not the grown-up toys, not the retirement investments, not the hobby, not even family. Sweet as it all may be, it cannot quite quench this particular thirst.

Saint Augustine, the great fifth-century Christian theologian from North Africa, came to faith after years of intellectual and spiritual wandering. He had lived a life that he had tried to fill with everything from rigorous scholarship to serious partying. Eventually, he would come to pray, "Our hearts are restless until they find their rest in Thee." Others have imagined a "God-shaped" void inside every human being.

Fifteen hundred years later, the American novelist Walker Percy battled a cynicism and depression that nearly pulled him under in his twenties. He ached for more, and at the age of thirty-one came to faith. He was baptized and confirmed on the same day as three hundred schoolchildren. Walker Percy, great man of letters, towered over that procession of twelve-year-olds, not minding a bit being led into the church by children.

An Indonesian friend of mine once said to me, "We Asians must have two stomachs. One is for regular food—vegetables, meat, fish, and fruit. The other stomach is for rice. No matter how much we eat, if we do not have rice, we are still hungry." Remembering an echo of something I had once heard, I thought to myself, if Jesus had been an Asian, I'll bet he would have said, "I am the rice of the world."

When people of faith are at their most candid, they acknowledge the very thing that many of us are often too proud to admit. Some longing once led them to look deeper and ask the underneath questions about life. They may speak about the questions that set them on the road. They may speak of their journey itself and a trust they have formed in the One who pulled them beyond the constricting boundaries of self and set them on a road to more.

Chapter 3

Finding or Found?

C. S. Lewis, Oxford don and resolute atheist, became a Christian in his middle years. He would write some of the most popular Christian literature ever penned, including an autobiography of his early years and later conversion to Christianity titled *Surprised by Joy*. In this book he makes it clear that he was quite comfortable in his atheism. Not only didn't he "find God," he wasn't even looking. God, Lewis says, found him. "Amiable agnostics will talk cheerfully about 'man's search for God.' To me, as I was then, they might as well have talked about the mouse's search for the cat."[1]

People speculate about "the search for God" as if the Transcendent One were a set of misplaced car keys. The awkward truth is that it is we who have misplaced ourselves. The journey of faith is not so much to "find God" as it is to struggle to follow a God who finds us. It would have sounded comic to Old Testament Hebrews to talk about a "quest for God." They spoke of being "chosen" and were not always pleased at the honor. It was clear to them that they were not selected on account of any supposed virtue or theological brilliance; rather, they were the people through whom God chose to articulate the divine purpose for reasons known only to God. God seems to have "found" them among all the people of the ancient world.

Likewise, Jesus' disciples don't appear to have been God-haunted religious searchers. When he found them, not a one of them was at prayer in the synagogue. They were not searching for God; they were at their nets and counting tables and happy enough to be there. The apostle Paul was hardly on a quest for deeper spirituality when he was knocked to his knees by the voice of Jesus on the road to Damascus.

He was a confident defender of the religious status quo on his way to arrest some nettlesome followers of this Jesus.

The eighteenth-century preacher and hymn writer John Newton had run away to sea as a boy and for years plied the ghastly slave trade between Africa and the Americas. He was anything but a spiritual quester, naming himself a "dissolute sailor." It was a chance reading of Thomas à Kempis's devotional classic, *The Imitation of Christ*, that first disquieted him and then set him on a journey he had never thought to make. It led to Christian faith, ministry, participation in the movement to abolish the slave trade, and the writing of several thousand hymns. With one exception, few of those hymns are sung today. But that one has become the most popular hymn in the English-speaking world: "Amazing grace, how sweet the sound, that saved a wretch like me! I once was lost, but now am found, was blind, but now I see."

No writer reflecting on the faith journey has made this point more eloquently than poet Francis Thompson. He named God "The Hound of Heaven" in the poem by the same name:

> I fled Him, down the nights and down the days;
>   I fled Him, down the arches of the years;
> I fled Him, down the labyrinthine ways
>   Of my own mind; and in the midst of tears
> I hid from Him, and under running laughter.
>   Up vistaed hopes I sped;
>   And shot, precipitated,
> Adown Titanic glooms of chasmed fear,
>   From those strong Feet that followed, followed after.[2]

When we are pursued by the events of our lives to ask the gnawing questions about the meaning of it all, it is none other than God who has been stirring the questions in us. The thirst we seek to quench is a gift from the very God who quenches the thirst. Struck still and incredulous before the grace and terror of creation, we can know that it is none other than the Creator who has planted the capacity to wonder in our souls. When we are made to go tête-à-tête with our vulnerability, it is God who whispers in the darkness. When we use our intellects to think our way into the possibility of faith, it is God who gave us a mind to reason in the first place. God is willing to use all things at hand to find us. The same C. S. Lewis who spoke of the mouse and the cat also complained of God's unapologetic use of "fine nets and strata-gems" to corner comfortable skeptics like himself.

Broadway has made Victor Hugo's classic nineteenth-century novel, *Les Misérables*, into common American cultural currency. Among other things, *Les Misérables* is a grand tale about a spiritual journey. That theme shines clear in a famous scene that casts its light across the whole of the novel. Jean Valjean, the novel's protagonist, is an ex-convict who has just been released after serving a sentence of nineteen years for stealing a loaf of bread. In the first chapter of the book, homeless and hungry, he is taken in by a kindly bishop and given a hot dinner and a bed for the night. He returns the favor with an act of larceny. In the middle of the night, he stuffs the bishop's silver into his bag and runs to the mountains. The police catch him and drag him back to the bishop's residence to confirm the theft. In one of the great scenes of French literature, three gendarmes surround Jean Valjean, head bowed in shame, and present him and the bag of purloined silver to the bishop. Before they can say a word, the bishop speaks to Jean Valjean: "Ah, there you are! . . . I'm glad to see you. But! I gave you the candlesticks also, which are silver like the rest. . . . Why did you not take them along with your plates?"[3] The incident transforms Jean Valjean, even though he had come with no interest in having his life transformed. He is haunted by this act of grace and, as the novel unfolds, led by it into his own life of grace. The man had been on no quest for anything more than a warm meal, a night's rest, and a sack of silver. But he had been sought and found by a compas-sion that left him dumbfounded and that altered the course of his life.

The faith road is not in search of a lost God but a way into a God who has passionately sought us, somehow found us, and then coaxed us onto the way. God "chooses" to call us to the road, not because we are particularly clever, notably ethical, or especially spiritual, but for reasons known only to God. In truth, many believers I have known—myself included—seem to be most unlikely choices.

Chapter 4

A Terrible Freedom

*T*he Gospels' story of Jesus' temptation in the wilderness, set just before he begins his ministry, is a sign of God's choice to guard our freedom, even while tirelessly pursuing us. The story stretches modern stunted imaginations to their limits. There is a stark and desert simplicity to the tale: The devil is the protagonist and a most beguiling character. No cloven-hoofed horned horror, this adversary is eminently reasonable.

He offers three reasonable temptations: First, he tempts Jesus with the power to make bread out of stones, bread that would not only have filled Jesus' empty stomach but would have meant enormous de facto power. Rome had long been keeping the restless masses of the capital city quiet with free bread. Next, he tempts Jesus with political power. Showing him the kingdoms of the world, he says, "To you I will give all this authority and glory." And then the third and strangest: As in a dream, the devil perches Jesus on the pinnacle of the great Temple in Jerusalem and says, "Jump, Jesus, jump." Then he quotes Scripture to the effect that surely God's angels would swoop down to break his fall. "Think, Jesus, think of the scene. You'll have them absolutely spellbound. Once they've seen a neat trick like that, they'll just have to believe in you."

Jesus first chooses not to manipulate with free bread. In that refusal we are shown a God who will not manipulate us into loyalty. Jesus then chooses not to commandeer obedience by brute force. In that refusal we are shown a God who will not compromise our freedom to win our trust. Finally, Jesus chooses not to coerce faith with a dramatic show of miracle. In that refusal we are shown a God who desires inward faith, not a faith pressed upon us. All three temptations are one. In refusing them, Jesus embodies a God who, even while pursuing us, will respect our freedom to choose.

In Fyodor Dostoyevsky's novel *The Brothers Karamazov*, in a story within a story known as "The Grand Inquisitor," the author imagines that Christ has returned to earth during the terror of the Inquisition. The Inquisition was, of course, a diabolical exercise in power of the very kind to which Christ said no. The Grand Inquisitor has had Christ arrested and may execute him. The Inquisitor knows who he is but bitterly reviles him: "Thou didst desire man's free love, that he should follow Thee freely. . . . In place of the rigid ancient law, man must hereafter with free heart decide for himself what is good. . . . Thou wouldst not enslave man with a miracle and didst crave faith freely given."

The Grand Inquisitor ends his harangue by saying,

> "Know that I fear Thee not. Know that I too have been in the wilderness. I too prized the freedom with which Thou hast blessed men. But I awakened and would not serve madness. I turned back and joined the ranks of those who have corrected Thy work. . . . I shall burn Thee for coming to hinder us. . . ."
>
> When the Inquisitor ceased speaking he waited some time for the Prisoner to answer him. His silence weighed down upon him. He saw that the Prisoner had listened intently all the time, looking gently in his face and evidently not wishing to reply. The old man longed for Him to say something, however bitter and terrible. But he suddenly approached the old man in silence and softly kissed him on his bloodless aged lips. That was all his answer.[1]

There is this delicate balance between the sovereign power of God on the one hand, and human freedom on the other. Both are true to our experience: the God who pursues us as insistently as a cat after a mouse, and our terrible freedom to turn away from this persistently loving God. But God refuses to exercise the kind of power that coerces faith, and in that choice guards our freedom. Mind you, this God of freedom seems stubbornly averse to taking no for an answer. This God inquires after us tirelessly and tiresomely, knocking sometimes softly, sometimes loudly, but always insistently.

Chapter 5

The Risk Involved

*T*rust and belief. Heart and head. Subjective faith and objective faith. In order for faith to be faith, it has to be a coin minted on both sides. A new gold dollar that might somehow come off the press stamped on but one side would be nabbed in quality control. *Belief about* God must be on one side; *trust in* God on the other. Both sides of the coin are needed for an integrated faith. If your faith is in your head only, it will eventually ossify into an arid and lifeless religiosity. If your faith is in your heart only, it will eventually devolve into some amorphous and impulsive spirituality. Without cognitive roots, faith withers. Without the solidity of the concrete—Scripture, theology, and creed—faith will dissipate into a shapeless fog of fleeting religious feelings. Such a pious fog will be blown about by every personal whim and passing spiritual fad until it has thinned to nothing.

The trust side of faith implies risk, and it is into risk that faith takes its first steps. Complement each other as they do, *trust in* usually walks a few steps in front of *belief about*. For example, Jesus' call to his disciples seems to come out of the blue. He happens upon them mending their fishing nets or sitting at a tax official's desk and simply says, "Follow me." And they make their decision as abruptly as the invitation is issued. There are no new-member classes, no orientation sessions, no discussion about where they might be going. The Gospels, of course, make no pretense of recording every word spoken by Jesus or his followers. You might guess that more was said. Nevertheless, these call stories were told in their abruptness for a reason. The spiritual fact they hold in their leanness is this: In the last analysis, the decision to take to the road is always made without all the facts. His first followers took

15

to the road because they were first captured by some divine intuition. That is, their faith was first a matter of the heart. The same is usually true for you and me. We don't set off on this road because we understand everything about the One we follow. We set off because there is something compelling about him that we cannot yet organize intellectually.

Anselm, the great medieval theologian, coined a venerable three-word Latin motto that still echoes around theology: *fides quaerens intellectum*, "faith seeking understanding." The seventeenth-century French philosopher and mathematician Blaise Pascal spoke of faith as "the wager." Others have talked about "the leap of faith." Faith is indeed first a wager, a leap, a risk, a commitment made without all the facts. It is this way for two good reasons.

First, in matters pertaining to God you never know everything or even close to everything. The spiritual writer Henri Nouwen once said, "You can be an expert in many things, but you can never be an expert in God." Neither our best theology nor our most studious biblical scholarship can ever wrap themselves around the vastness of God. Our sharpest human "small-*t* truths" are never the same thing as the eternal "capital-*t* Truth" of God. The greatest religious thinkers have always understood this. It has always been lightweights who fell into believing that their ideas about God were the same as the real thing. In his fine book *The Trivialization of God*, Don McCullough put it this way: "Once the last plank of our theological house has been firmly nailed down, we may discover that the only god we have contained is too trivial to be worth the effort."[1]

The great medieval theologian Thomas Aquinas,

> after completing his thirty-eight treatises, three thousand articles, and the ten thousand objections of his *Summa Theologica* . . . abruptly quit his work on the 6th of December, 1273. He had had a profound experience while at worship and announced to his secretary that he would write no more. "I can do no more," he tried to explain. "Such things have been revealed to me that all I have written seems to me as so much straw."[2]

The twentieth-century Swiss theologian Karl Barth, whose monumental opus *Church Dogmatics* is twice as long as all Aquinas wrote, said that he imagined that he would enter heaven with a pushcart filled with his books and that the angels would laugh at him. "Indeed," Barth said, "I shall be able to dump even the *Church Dogmatics* . . . on some heavenly floor as a pile of waste paper."[3]

The second reason that faith begins with risk is more subtle but just as crucial. Not only can God never be fully comprehended, but the ironic truth is that much if not most of what you might come to perceive about God can be encountered only in the very act of following God. The deepest understanding of things spiritual is hidden from the eyes of those who do not risk the spiritual road. The road itself is the teacher. You try faith on like you put on a new pair of glasses, not knowing what you might see until you wear them. Then you move through the world wearing lenses that make everything appear sharp and fresh but strange and differently shaped. You risk the new perspective of faith, you dare to look at life, watch the flow of the days, and read Scripture through these new and disorienting lenses of faith. You pray when you are still unsure of prayer. You may worship even though you have only the most tenuous spiritual grasp of the One you praise.

But once you have taken the heart-led leap, once you trust and follow that subjective, divine intuition, then the shapelessness of intuition comes to be carved into a shape by concrete words and grounded concepts. Here enter theology, Bible study, the reading of books, the saying of creeds and catechisms—the *belief about* side of the coin. These are words, concepts, and ancient images of God tested by time and Spirit that give shape and substance to the vagaries of intuition. Trust moves a step at a time deeper into understanding; slowly heart and head take hand; trust and belief kiss.

I have known a few people who came to faith because they believed—cognitively believed—that faith was intellectually necessary before they had a subjective trust in the Divine, people whose heads led the way into faith, their hearts bringing up the rear. Such "understanding seeking faith" is not unheard of, but it is the rarer way in. More often, faith is first a risk. As with Jesus' disciples, you drop your nets and follow. After three years on the road you may be able to answer the question Jesus finally asked Peter: "Who do you say that I am?"

There may be much you doubt as you sit in church and dread the moment the congregation rises to say the Apostles' Creed. You glance to your right and to your left, looking to see if your neighbors in the pew will speak the words easily or awkwardly. Perhaps when the time comes, they can say it and believe it for you, at least for now. Or maybe there is a word in the creed you can believe that the old man in front of you cannot wrap his head around today. But together—as a community—we believe.

A church history professor at Yale Divinity School once invited an Orthodox priest to be a guest lecturer. He offered a dry talk on the history of the creeds, at the end of which an earnest student asked, "Father Theodore, what can one do when one finds it impossible to affirm certain tenets of the creed?" The priest looked confused. "Well, you just say it. It's not that hard to master. With a little effort, most can learn it by heart."

"No, you don't understand," continued the student, "what am I to do when I have difficulty affirming parts of the creed—like the Virgin Birth?" The priest still looked confused. "You just say it. It will come to you eventually."

The frustrated student now pleaded, "How can I with integrity affirm a creed in which I do not believe?"

"It's not your creed, young man!" said the priest. "It's our creed. Keep saying it, for heaven's sake! Eventually, it may come to you. For some, it takes longer than for others. How old are you? Twenty-three? Don't be so hard on yourself. There are lots of things that you don't know at twenty-three. Eventually, it may come to you. Even if it doesn't, don't worry."[4]

Albert Schweitzer's genius revealed itself early in life and set him on a dazzling career that ranged from theology to the arts. At the age of twenty-six, he wrote a book on Jesus and the Bible that shook the theological establishment of the late nineteenth century to its core. He became one of the greatest organists of his time and wrote a volume on Bach that is still a definitive work on that great musician. He became assistant pastor of a middle-class parish in Strasbourg and might have been the master organist of Europe. He could have settled into a position on the theological faculty in a lovely city in south Germany or spent his days as pastor of a comfortable congregation in Strasbourg. Instead, he chose to go back to school, study medicine, and go to a place called Lambaréné in French Equatorial Africa. There, in a remoteness that the world of today no longer knows, he lived out his life offering free medical treatment to the poor.

Schweitzer wrote these words about the risky decision to follow the Jesus we come to know only in the act of following:

He comes to us as One unknown, without a name, as of old, by the lake-side, He came to those men who knew Him not. He speaks to us the same word: "Follow thou Me!" and sets us to the tasks which He has to fulfil for our time. He commands. And to those who obey Him, whether they be wise or simple, He will reveal Himself in the toils, the conflicts, the sufferings which they shall pass through in His fellowship, and, as an ineffable mystery, they shall learn in their own experience who He is.[5]

PART II

The Way

Chapter 6

Beside Yourself

I Believe in God

*T*ony Campolo is a liberal evangelical Italian Baptist from Philadelphia. That description alone would be enough to make anything he might say intriguing. He is also an earthy and riveting preacher. In a sermon, Tony once told a story that began with him driving on the Schuylkill Expressway through the middle of Philadelphia. Roads like the Schuylkill Expressway exist nowhere but in Philadelphia, thank goodness: two narrow lanes with no shoulders, concrete barriers eighteen inches from your right rearview mirror, ten times as much traffic as the road was designed for in 1928.

Tony said he was driving on the Schuylkill at rush hour on a blistering day when he got a flat tire. There was no shoulder, so he just stopped in the middle of the right-hand lane to change it. It turned out to be no quick job. He was listening to the car radio as he struggled with the jack and the tire iron and the lug nuts. The radio program was suddenly interrupted with a special bulletin, a traffic alert. An apocalyptic radio voice announced that rush hour all over Philadelphia was at a veritable standstill. There was some as-yet-unidentified problem on the Schuylkill. At that moment, Tony said, he looked up to see a TV traffic helicopter hovering over him aiming its mobile camera down at his tire-changing operation. He said that the first thought to enter his mind at that moment was, "It's me! I, Tony Campolo, have tied up the whole city of Philadelphia. I, Tony Campolo, am a traffic congestion superstar."

If the brokenness of this old world could be said to have a single cause, some core malignancy, it must be this tendency, part of our common humanity, for each of us to see himself or herself as the center of the universe. As every parent knows, such is the approximate world-view of most two-year-olds. It is a normal spiritual vantage point for small children most of the time and most adults a lot of the time. Each of us identifies himself or herself as the one around which everyone and everything else rotate like planets around the sun. In this altogether too common view of things, every event is judged according to its effect on you at the center. Other people are valued for their emotional or material usefulness. Things are judged good or bad not by some external or absolute standard but by how they might help or hinder you and your purposes. In such a moral universe of self-orientation, every-thing can become self-serving. Even religion can devolve into narcis-sistic spirituality, a way to find peace . . . for *me*, a way to find fulfillment . . . for *me*, a way to discover meaning . . . for *me*. From a geometric point of view, this proclivity to plant one's self at the cen-ter of existence makes perfect sense. From my position, there is infin-ity to the east, infinity to the west, infinity to the south, infinity to the north, infinity upward, and infinity downward. It's only logical: I must be the center of everything.

That crusty theologian and writer of mystery novels Dorothy Say-ers observes that this self-orientation is so basic that it percolates into our language. With her tongue slightly in cheek, she notes how absurd it is for a person who is late for a meeting to walk into the room and offer as an excuse the fact that on the way there he or she took the "wrong road." What do you mean, "wrong road"? Sayers notes that there is obviously nothing wrong with the road, that it's a fine road and clearly going to the right place. "The road wasn't wrong," she concludes, "the driver was wrong. . . ."

To permit God to trespass into this tidy universe with self at the center will invite no end of mischief. A God in the picture will do nothing less than turn this human proclivity toward self-orientation on its head. In time, that which once seemed "only natural" and "right side up" will be seen for the moral and spiritual inversion it is. I warn you: To permit God through the door will radically reorient your spir-itual and moral universe. Not I, but the One who transcends me becomes the point of orientation. Not I, but the One whom faith names God comes to be the nexus of meaning. Not I, but God it is who gives shape and purpose to all things. God becomes the One from whom we come, the One unto whom we return, and the One in whom we live and move and have our being.

To take to the road of faith is to set off on a way that will end up tugging us out of a "me-at-the-center" schematic of the universe. Ironically, the very reorientation we fear is precisely what we long for: One who is radically other, beyond us, and whose very being denies us that position as "sun of our own solar system." Any true geography that places divinity on the map must place God at the center. A God plotted around me at the map's center cannot be God at all.

Jesus was once asked, "What is the greatest commandment in the law?" The law the questioner referred to was the collection of hundreds of rules about ethical and daily behavior that governed life in his Jewish world. Jesus' two-part answer, known as the Great Commandment, speaks to the heart of this matter of orientation to God and the place of others and of the self. Jesus said, "'You shall love the Lord your God with all your heart, and with all your soul, and with all your mind.' This is the greatest and first commandment." The orientation of this love implies the redirecting of the self toward God at the center that we have been discussing. But the second part of the commandment underscores the infinite value, not only of other human beings, but also of the self that does the turning. Jesus next said, "And a second is like it: 'You shall love your neighbor as yourself.'" To "love your neighbor" is to regard and treat other human beings as equally beloved of God. Those last words of the commandment, "as yourself," remind us that it is also natural, healthy, and morally right to love one's self.

Some years ago, a well-meaning friend gave me a paperback book by a popular religious writer more famous for depth of piety than profundity of theology. Many of its pages included pictures, diagrams actually, offered to illustrate the point of the words on the page. They showed stick figures in various poses, arrows pointing this way and that, and assorted interlocking circles. It laid out Christianity like ninth-grade geometry. Early in the book the author proffered two diagrams to show the "before" and "after" of conversion to faith. Both had a simple throne at the center of the drawing. In the "before" version, a stick figure is perched on the throne, its feet dangling off the ground and a too-large crown set above its head. Around the throne is a circle of other stick figures, all oriented toward the throne at the center. An arrow points to the figure at the center identifying it as "YOU." In the "after" diagram, a cross now wearing the crown is set above the throne, which is again surrounded by a circle of stick people, one of whom, no larger than the others, is pointed out by an arrow as "YOU." I remember a sophisticated smirk crossing my face as I turned to the next page. "Such naiveté," I thought to myself all those years ago. Such simplicity, indeed. Unforgettable simplicity. I threw the book away thirty years ago, but I can still see the drawings on that page as if they had been printed like film on the back of my eyeballs.

We live in a world that often seems unapologetically self-absorbed. We walk through it as individuals only too ready to blend into that culture and see ourselves as little centers of our private universes. So it should hardly be a surprise if moving off the throne can be painful. And of course, it is a procedure that is never totally successful. The New Testament speaks of this surrender of self and turning to God in the jarring, razor-sharp vocabulary of "cross" and "death." Jesus starkly declares, "If any want to become my followers, let them deny themselves and take up their cross and follow me. For those who want to save their life will lose it, and those who lose their life for my sake will find it" (Matt. 16:24–25). To "take up the cross" is to reject that positioning of self at the center of the cosmos.

The apostle Paul uses language every bit as deliberately disturbing. Time and again, he speaks of "dying with Christ," or "dying to sin," a reorientation so radical that only this startling vocabulary can speak the honest truth. These are discomforting words, but they speak of what has to be. The fact is that if we occupy the center, God cannot. The cross is "death to self" and is absolutely necessary if God is to occupy the nexus of our orientation. Everything in us that demands to be the center must die. And only when it dies can we live in a new orientation toward God at the center.

As ancient, powerful, and personally applicable as this image of faith as a "turning from self to God" may be, there are many people in the world for whom it does not fit. Impoverished and oppressed people, women pressed into veritable slavery in radically male-dominated societies, even men and women in our prosperous modern world who are weighed down by low self-esteem, do not need to be told that their beleaguered self must "die" when it is in fact already being killed daily. For many people, turning to God may actually begin with an affirmation of the inestimable value of the self. Faith begins not so much with removing the "me" from a throne on which it has never been perched, but rather begins with taking a dignified and respectable place among that circle of "stick people" around the throne. For many, what dies in Paul's rhetoric of "dying to sin" is not exactly the self, but rather the self's habit of buying into patterns of oppression, humiliation, or self-loathing.

Indeed, this caveat serves as an important reminder to the most self-regarding of us. Turning away from self and reorienting life toward God—"that which is not me"—does not mean that my self is demeaned; rather the turning directs me to find an equal place among my peers in humanity, side by side in our common orientation to the One who is at the center.

For two millennia, Christians have marked the beginning of the faith journey with the sacrament of baptism. It is the ancient initiation of those committed to the Way. Water speaks of the gift of life, for all life is nourished by water. Water bespeaks cleansing, the forgiveness of God who forgives and will forgive time and again in the years to come. Water speaks of crossings into new country—all the biblical rivers forded along those ancient journeys—crossings that foreshadow the entry of the one being baptized into new land. But harder to hear are the words that speak of baptism as death—death to self and reorientation to God. "Do you not know," Paul dared to ask the Romans, "that all of us who have been baptized into Christ Jesus were baptized into his death? Therefore we have been buried with him by baptism into death, so that, just as Christ was raised from the dead by the glory of the Father, so we too might walk in newness of life" (Rom. 6:3–4).

The writer Will Campbell remembers his own baptism as a youngster in East Fork River in Mississippi. His parents had ordered him a new suit of clothes for the occasion from the Sears and Roebuck catalog. He was accompanied by his brother Joe, something of a youthful skeptic. Joe watched from the riverbank as several new Christians were immersed in the river. He grew increasingly worried for his brother's safety. Finally, he slid down the muddy bank and grabbed his brother, "Will, dear God, don't let them do this to you. A fellow could get killed doing this." Will Campbell later reflected, "It took me thirty years to recognize that was precisely the point."[1]

Such extreme and profound reorientation—being dead to self and alive to God—is radically more than mere assent to the intellectual idea of God. It is quite possible to affirm that God exists, as 90 percent of Americans do, and keep the real-life implications of that belief at arm's length. We are often stunningly stubborn about turning the faith coin over. We keep the *belief about* side faceup but avoid flipping it over to read *trust in*. We know that such trust implies both relationship and commitment, steps we often fear to take. Trust demands action and movement. You can believe that God exists—either because it is a reasonable intellectual assumption or because it was the creed you were taught—and never so much as set foot on the road.

The way home begins here, in the radical reorientation that is death to self-orientation. Only when that in us which clamors to be a little god is drowned in cool clear water can God be God and can we be who we are. In this death is hidden nothing less than liberation from a nasty little prison of self. Passing through this water, we are given an identity that frees us to be who we were created to be. Baptism frees us from the horror of having to be the center of the universe. God sets us in our place and then sets us on the road with a promise that we do not travel alone.

I sometimes thumb through old copies of the *New Yorker* just to read the cartoons. One engraved in my memory pictures two of the wealthy-looking tycoon types who seem to populate *New Yorker* cartoons. They are in double-breasted blazers, cocktails in hand, standing on the lawn of a magnificent estate overlooking the sea, doubtless somewhere in the Hamptons. One of them, gazing out over the water, says to the other, "Sometimes I wish someone else were Captain of my Fate and Master of my Soul." The good news is this: Somebody else is.

Chapter 7

Specifically Spiritual

I Believe in Jesus Christ

*I*n Aldous Huxley's novel *Those Barren Leaves*, a character named Miss Thriplow, who finds herself between affairs and bored, is suddenly taken with the idea that she ought to become more "serious and spiritual":

> She got into bed, and lying on her back, with all her muscles relaxed, she began to think about God. . . . *God is a spirit, she said to herself. She tried to picture something huge and empty, but alive. A huge flat expanse of sand, for example, and over it a huge blank dome of sky; and above the sand everything should be tremulous and shimmering with heat—emptiness that was yet alive. A spirit, an all-pervading spirit. God is a spirit. Three camels appeared on the horizon of the sandy plain and went lolloping along in an absurd, ungainly fashion from left to right. Miss Thriplow made an effort and dismissed them. God is a spirit, she said aloud. But of all animals, camels are really almost the queerest; when one thinks of their frightfully supercilious faces, with their protruding underlips like the last Hapsburg kings of Spain. . . . No, no; God is a spirit, all-pervading, everywhere. All the universes are made one in him.*[1]

Our well-intentioned world is entering the new millennium as famished for "spirituality" as well-intentioned Miss Thriplow. We too long to be more "serious and spiritual." In recent years, this cultural phenomenon has given rise to something of a "spirituality" growth industry. Often these new spiritualities are both rootless and amorphous. They range from the bizarre television spirituality of "Psychic Friends" to thoughtful but ultimately unsatisfying books outlining endless varieties of spiritual technique. If the word *God* comes up in such prescriptions, it is usually a-god-of-no-name. Sociologist Robert Bellah documented this rise of home-brewed spirituality in his book, *Habits of the Heart*. He illustrated the movement with the story of a young nurse he named Sheila who has since become something of an emblem of this new, self-generated kind of faith: "I believe in God," she told Bellah. "I'm not a religious fanatic. I can't remember the last time I went to church. My faith has carried me a long way. It's 'Sheilaism.' Just my own 'little voice.'"[2]

It is not only current pop-spirituality that has shied away from the concrete. Philosophers and theologians have sometimes leaned toward vague abstractions, often consummately elusive ones: Plato's notion of God as "Idea" and Aristotle's "Unmoved Mover," the father it would seem of the "Prime Mover" of the Enlightenment Deists. Tillich is somewhat more helpful with his "Ground of Being," more so than the theologian who suggested defining God as "Being as Such." Popular science fiction has played with images of God as everything from a stone monolith floating in the dark heart of space to a permeating "Force" (dare I capitalize the *f*?) diffuse in all the universe.

But the truth is that our mortal minds, shaped as they are by the earthy stuff we know, demand spirit-soil firm enough to hold roots. We are human beings molded and bounded by what we have seen, heard, smelled, touched, and tasted in our earthbound lives. The vagaries of shapeless spirituality without the concrete and particular to carve the ethereal into shape are never solid enough.

The good news is that in divine compassion for our earthliness, God has spoken a Word that mortal ears can hear, a Word spoken in the form of flesh and blood like us. Such is precisely what we long for—One who is radically other and beyond us, yet One whom we can come to know. To this world of hunger, Christian faith is so audacious as to proclaim a God who pushed through mystery veiled in mystery to reveal the Divine Self. Christian faith proclaims a God of scandalous specificity. It revels in a God who has revealed God's Self in the concreteness of time and space. This God has moved in the rough-and-tumble flow of history. God "spoke" in the story of the Old Testament Hebrews. In the fullness of time, God was so gracious as to speak a defining Word and become incarnate, enfleshed. In

Jesus of Nazareth, we encounter not a distant God of armchair speculation; rather, we come face to face with a God who speaks a Word we can begin to comprehend. At the heart of the insistently concrete Christian faith is this radical and scandalous affirmation that in Jesus of Nazareth, God is to be known. God is made known not just in the words Jesus spoke, but in his very being, in and through the living of his life, the manner of his death, and the final word of his resurrection.

The ironic fact, however, is that many people much prefer comfortably a distant and amorphous divinity to One who has come audaciously close. When God is but an idea, the Divine is safely confined inside the fence of what I would prefer God to be and what I can imagine God to be. I would imagine a God who is eminently manageable, manageable by me to my ends. A manageable divine abstraction is unlikely to ask much of me. One of my wittier friends names this comfy god-at-a-distance "the cosmic muffin." "It" would hardly ask anything of us as discomforting as discipleship, sacrifice, or intimacy.

Christians do of course affirm the transcendence of God. To do so is to remember that God is radically "other" and beyond the categories of human experience. We confess that our ability to conceive of God is always limited by mortal minds. We are simply not vast enough to think the vastness of God all the way through. Christians admit that even the most eloquent language is too earthbound to speak the highest and the deepest truth about the likes of the Divine.

However (and this is the great *however* of faith), Christians dare to affirm that this gulf between our limited humanity on the one hand, and the radical and transcendent otherness of God on the other, has been bridged by Jesus Christ. Robert Clyde Johnson, in his little book *The Meaning of Christ*, observed that this is such a daring affirmation for religious people who have long been insistent about the mystery and transcendence of God that it lies "on the ragged edge of blasphemy."

We who bear his name insist that Jesus is "like us" in our humanity. The Gospels are remarkably down-to-earth in their presentation of this Jewish carpenter who eats and drinks, walks the dusty roads of a backwater Roman province, tells stories about farmers and crafty businessmen, loves and heals, and dies a criminal's death. Yet, the brazen Christian claim is that in him and through him, we come to encounter God in such a powerful way that we dare to claim that this same Galilean peasant named Jesus *is* God. Paul captured the irony of incarnation in the second chapter of Philippians when he wrote of Jesus: " . . . who, though he was in the form of God, did not regard equality with God as something to be exploited, but emptied himself, taking the form of a slave, being born in human likeness."

The reformer Martin Luther was insistent that God's naked majesty could never be beheld directly. "So," he said, "in order to shield human beings from the unapproachable light of God's glory, God always remains hidden behind a mask." But the mask is that of the ordinary, the mask of an ordinary human being in whom we can see the shape of the face that the mask hides. All of this lies at the border of poetic hyperbole, but it reminds us that we can only apprehend what we can imagine on the basis of our experience as human beings. We are human and we are finite, so we must understand the Divine and the Infinite in the terms of humanity and finitude.

In the center of London lies Trafalgar Square. It commemorates the battle of Trafalgar, one of the great naval battles of history, which was fought in the Mediterranean off the coast of North Africa in October 1805. It pitted the combined French and Spanish fleet of Napoleon Bonaparte against the British fleet under the command of a man who was already the most beloved of all British heroes, Admiral Lord Horatio Nelson. The British defeated the French and Spanish. The event was a turning point in the Napoleonic Wars and gave Britain control of the seas. But Lord Nelson was killed in the battle; his body was returned to England and buried in St. Paul's Cathedral.

At the center of Trafalgar Square a towering monolith was erected in honor of Lord Nelson. And at the top of the column they placed a statue of the great man. But the statue was so high that Nelson was invisible from ground level; you could see nothing of him "up there"; he was lost in the heavens. So they did the only thing they could do. They brought Nelson down here. In 1948, an exact replica of the statue at the top of the monolith was erected at eye level where it could be clearly seen. So also Christ in his incarnation brings God down from the top of heaven's pillars to street level.

By another metaphor, one might even understand Christ as the window through whom we see with clarity into God. The Spanish philosopher Ortega y Gasset, in reflecting on how to view modern art, noted that such art is like a window through which we see a garden. If we focus our vision only or mostly on the window, its frames and the glass, the garden beyond is blurred. But if we look through the window to the garden in the distance, the garden comes into clear view and the window itself comes to serve its proper function, which is to be seen through.

Jesus does not just show us the road, he is himself the road. "I am the way, and the truth, and the life," he said. This is much more than if he had said, "I will lead you in the way, teach you the truth, and show you how to live." As if the incarnation were not scandalous enough, Christians also insist that just as his life discloses truth about God, so also his death reveals God's way with humanity. It's important to remember that each of the four Gospels devotes a huge proportion of its pages to the last few days of Jesus' life and the details surrounding his death. The apostle Paul, author of the majority of the letters in the New Testament, has much more to say about the meaning of Jesus' death than he does about the life and teachings of Jesus. The Christian faith has from its very beginnings stubbornly insisted that the whole story of Jesus necessarily encompasses not only his life but also the offense that was his death and the mystery that is his resurrection.

It is, of course, easier to understand how a life has meaning than how an unjust and brutal judicial murder does. The Gospels clearly say that Jesus came to understand that death waited for him in Jerusalem and that this death was purposeful. He says little, however, about precisely why death must come to him as it will or exactly how it would be meaningful. It's also clear that his followers soon came to believe that his death, like his life, revealed truth about God. Beginning in the New Testament itself, Christians began to explore vocabularies and theories to understand Jesus' death.

Rooted at the heart of the Christian faith is the stubborn declaration that Jesus "died for us." Precisely why his death came to mean so much to Christians has, however, been a subject of wonderful and diverse exploration over the ages. The twentieth-century Christian writer and apologist C. S. Lewis noted that the exact meaning of Jesus' death would always lie beyond theories about its meaning when he wrote, "The central Christian belief is that Christ's death has somehow put us right with God and given us a fresh start. Theories as to how it did this are another matter. A good many different theories have been held as to how it works; what all Christians are agreed on is that it does work."[3]

Christians have come to trust that *somehow* by his death on the cross, Jesus spans the divide between human and the divine. Christians have come to believe that *somehow* by his death on the cross, he bridges the moral chasm between our imperfection and God's perfection. The ideas explored by Jesus' first followers and then hammered out later by generation upon generation of Christians are often called "theories of the atonement," even though the term *atonement* is relatively recent.

It was not invented until the sixteenth century, by compressing two English words, *at* and *one,* and tacking on the Latin suffix *-ment.* It originally meant simply "agreement" or even "peace." Obviously, neither Jesus nor Paul, nor medieval theologians, nor most Reformation thinkers for that matter would have known the term. Nevertheless, *atonement* has become the modern umbrella word for the variety of perceptions of the meaning of Jesus' death.

Christians have come to understand the "how" in the "somehow" power of Jesus' death in three general ways: forgiveness, inspiration, and revelation. The first cluster of atonement theories understands the cross in terms of human sinfulness and God's forgiveness. The second group of atonement theories understands Jesus' sacrifice in terms of how it inspires his followers to similar acts of love, integrity, and self-denial. The third way of understanding Jesus' death sees it in terms of the way it shows the depth of God's love for us and God's readiness to be with us in suffering.

Atonement theories, from the New Testament era to the twenty-first century, have always been couched in words and ideas that made sense to people at the time. But often, as vocabularies and worldviews shifted, an understanding of Jesus' death that one generation of Christians found profoundly meaningful gradually became remote, even senseless or offensive to another generation.

For instance, most of the first followers of Jesus were Jews rooted in a religious culture that understood the human relationship to God in terms of purity or cleanliness. In this religious system, a person could become close to God by keeping purity laws that made you ritually clean. It was not just moral behavior that guarded your personal purity, but also what you ate or did not eat, how you washed, and with whom you sat at table.

The first Jewish Christians were also accustomed to a theology that assumed that sins were forgiven only by the shedding of blood, specifically the blood of animals sacrificed in the Temple of Jerusalem. So it was natural that they would come to understand the death of Jesus in the familiar terms of Temple sacrifice and ritual cleanliness. The Letter to the Hebrews was written by and for such Christians, and it quite naturally interprets the death of Jesus in the then-evocative terms of sacrifice and cleansing. It made perfect theological and moral sense to a Jewish Christian in the first century. But as powerful as this vocabulary was, images of blood sacrifice and ritual purity have become foreign, if not offensive, to many modern Christians.

At the end of the eleventh century, a theologian named Anselm developed a theory of the atonement that still influences the way many Christians understand the meaning of the death of Jesus. Anselm's early medieval context shaped his worldview and molded his way of understanding the cross. To Anselm and his world, the essential dilemma that the cross addressed was the offense that human sinfulness caused to the honor of God. The honor of a feudal lord or monarch was a matter of immediate relevance to an eleventh-century European. Just as a feudal serf's theft of his sovereign's property was understood not only as larceny, but as an offense to the honor of the lord of the manor, the scandalous behavior of God's subjects was understood as an insult to the divine Lord that demanded to be set right. Divine honor and integrity insisted that there be rectification, and rectification implied the punishment of offending humanity.

But, Anselm reasoned, just as God cannot overlook the offense of human behavior and remain God, God's mercy simply cannot stand for the destruction of the very humanity God loves even though humans really ought to pay the price. In any case, Anselm said, the offense of human sinfulness is so great that only God could ever pay the price. Jesus, who was both God and human, lived a life of such value that he and he alone can satisfy justice and set the order of the universe right.

His death saves humanity from the destruction that the perfect justice of God demands. So, according to Anselm's reasoning, by his death Jesus takes our place; he is "substituted" for us, hence the common name of Anselm's theory and its descendants, "substitutionary atonement." Anselm's theory was clear and consistent to a medieval mind imbued with feudal concepts of honor and satisfaction. It has been refashioned by later generations of theologians and is still both evocative and normative to many Christians. However, to other modern believers it has come to be a distant, curious, even repellent way to understand Jesus' death.[4]

Both of these theories of the atonement are part of the first of the three ways of perceiving the death of Jesus because they understand it in terms of the forgiveness of sin. It is important to note that these three views of the atonement—forgiveness, inspiration, and revelation—are by no means mutually exclusive. Indeed, at different points in life's journey, a Christian may ache for an understanding of Jesus' death that offers forgiveness radical enough to forgive what may seem unforgivable. In another life passage, a believer may find inspiration in the integrity and courage that led Jesus to the cross. And again, in the midst of suffering, Christians have been comforted by the cross's revolutionary and revelatory declaration that God is not aloof from us in pain, loss, and disorientation, but suffers with us.

The Cross as Forgiveness

Jesus speaks but twice of his impending death in relationship to forgiveness. In the twentieth chapter of Matthew's Gospel, as he turns his face toward Jerusalem and the looming cross, he says, "The Son of man came not to be served but to serve, and to give his life as a ransom for many." On the night before his death, gathered with his disciples for the Passover meal that Christians will later celebrate as Holy Communion, he says, "This is my blood of the new covenant, which is poured out for many for the forgiveness of sins."

In several of his letters in the New Testament, Paul echoes this theme by introducing new images connecting Jesus' death and God's forgiveness. A variety of metaphors come into play, many of them peculiar to their time and place. The cross is understood as *reconciliation,* bringing peace among people alienated from God and one another. It's called a *ransom,* implying that humanity has been kidnapped by evil. Images of *redemption* suggest the purchase of freedom for a humanity enslaved by sin. Echoing passages in the Old

Testament book of Isaiah, Christians began to speak of the way in which Jesus' suffering brings *healing*. The book of Hebrews introduces jarring images of *cleansing* and *sacrifice*. Linking the cross to Easter, other images understand the cross and resurrection together as the decisive *victory* in the cosmic conflict between good and evil, life and death.

Later thinkers would expand on all these biblical images of forgiveness and reconciliation between God and humanity, often formalizing them into systematic, even tidy and rigid theories. Christian tradition has always insisted that somehow Jesus' death illustrates the depth of human sinfulness, and somehow it then enacts or effects the radical forgiveness of God. But no single understanding of how this works has always been normative or essential. Somehow, through the death of Jesus, forgiveness becomes real. Somehow.

The Cross as Inspiration

When Anselm was formalizing his "cross as forgiveness" theology in the vocabulary of substitutionary atonement, a younger contemporary was thinking through the meaning of Jesus' death in a very different way. Abelard, a popular priest and teacher at Notre Dame Cathedral in Paris, found Anselm's reasoning outrageous. He thought it "cruel and wicked" that the justice of God would demand shedding the blood of an innocent to bring about forgiveness. He worked out a distinctly different understanding of Jesus' death that saw it as an enactment of God's unrelenting love for undeserving humanity, a love so powerful that "our hearts should be enkindled by such a gift of divine grace" and by this example be inspired to "true charity" that "should not now shrink from doing anything for him." Abelard's thinking and similar understandings of the atonement have often been called "moral influence theories."[5]

Jesus himself spoke in similar terms when he challenged his followers to take up their cross and follow him, a stark image of self-denial inspired by Jesus' self-sacrifice. Christians have sometimes understood the cross as the inevitable result of Jesus' conflict with a rigid and oppressive power structure. In the deadly showdown with local and Roman imperial power that last week in Jerusalem, the choice before Jesus was either cross or compromise. By this understanding, his death becomes a sign of his integrity and an inspiration to his followers to live lives of similar consistency and courage in the face of oppression and injustice.

The Cross as Revelation

At its simplest—so obvious we're likely to look past it—the death of Jesus is, like the life of Jesus, an event that reveals to us the way of God with the world. The cross by this theory, so basic that it is hardly theory, simply discloses the heart of God, or, in more traditional theological language, its "revelation" of central truth about the Divine.

The cross most clearly discloses two interrelated truths. First, the cross portrays in starkest terms a love so vast as to descend to any depth for the sake of beloved humanity. Second, the cross is a sign that God has passed through the very suffering that is intrinsically bound up with the human condition. The death of Jesus becomes enactment of God's love for us and presence with us even in the anguished depths of our experience.

The cross never permits Christian faith to be naive about suffering, injustice, and loss. Planted squarely at the center of the story is this high-water mark of evil's flood tide, silently insisting that our faith goes as deep as human experience goes. In the death of Jesus, God descends into human suffering and incorporates—takes in God's corpus, God's body—the whole of mortal brokenness and pain. On the cross, God becomes our sure companion for every step of the journey, bright and overcast, fair and stormy. By the death of Jesus, God tells us, "There is no pain that you might bear that I have not borne, no darkness that can overshadow you that I have not seen, no fear that might grip you that I have not known. I have been there and I am with you."

Several years ago a friend named John and I were moving furniture from the apartment of another church member, an elderly widow named Helen, who had just made a wrenching decision to move into a nursing home. Helen had given my daughter Grace the old bedroom set that we were lugging out of her garden apartment. The rest was going to the Salvation Army. Helen had slept surrounded by this department-store veneered bedroom suite all her life. She had no children to leave it to. It was a grim moving day, emptying rooms stuffed with memory into John's borrowed truck.

Each trip from the apartment to the curb set John and me to thinking about the melancholy of it all—an old woman despondent about her move and a life of memories about to be sold on the cheap. We were about to carry the old bedstead out to the truck, John on one end and I on the other, when he suddenly said something that startled me. John was a junior high shop teacher, a Long Island Italian, blunt, anything but talkative, and certainly not given to self-disclosure. In a few lean and carefully chosen words he told me about the death of his infant child more than a decade earlier, long before I knew him. I had been told the story, but we had never discussed it. John talked about the anguish that he and his wife had passed through. I knew them both as upbeat, dogged church members who taught the junior high class that everybody else dodged and showed up for every church cleanup day. They were also the doting parents of a son and a daughter, born on either side of their dead child. I asked the question that came first to my mind. "How did you get through it?" John was silent for a moment. He set down his end of the bedstead and looked at me. Then he nodded to the heavens and said, "He's been there; that's all there is to say. God's been there." Then he picked up his end of Helen's bed and we carried it to the truck.

Somehow the death of Jesus, an event that might have been just another installment in the sorry human epic of torture, injustice, and death come too soon, is transformed by resurrection and becomes a death with meaning. Somehow, this death bears forgiveness; somehow this death inspires; somehow this death discloses the boundless love of God, a love so unbounded that it willingly suffers with us. Somehow on the cross, the love of God reaches across the chasm gouged between humanity and the Divine and pulls us across into eternally outstretched arms. Somehow.

As the cross promises reconciliation with God, the resurrection is God's assurance that Jesus is more than a mere memory. Through the mystery of Easter, God not only declares the obvious, namely, that God is stronger than death. Easter also promises that for those who would follow him, Jesus is not merely a founder to be remembered but a continuing and living presence. Jesus is not simply a man who once taught in ancient Galilee and once mirrored God to long-dead peasants and fishermen. Many movements, even religions, have such founders. Jesus is not so much the founder of Christianity as he is its living, breathing life. Resurrection is the enacted promise that death is not the last word. But Easter is also the enacted declaration that Jesus Christ is a living Presence with whom we can be in spiritual relationship.

In summary, only in a secondary sense can the Christian faith itself be called "the Way," even though it was actually so named before it was called Christianity. Christian faith is a "religion" in the sense that it contains an ancient body of teaching, rituals, and daily practices that have shaped the lives of men and women for two thousand years. But Jesus is not simply a teacher, another source of spiritual truths. It would hardly be especially good news if Jesus had done no more than introduce one more set of religious rules and practices to the world. In the end, the good news is that Jesus himself, more than any religion, is the Way, a living Way into life with God.

Chapter 8

Present Tense Divinity

I Believe in the Holy Spirit

*E*ven if I believe that Jesus lives, the fact is that he is not sitting at my kitchen table. If God is real, "theoretically" real is insufficient. God must be actually real to us in our time and our place. In the first chapter of part 2, we noted that since the advent of time humanity has longed for that which is beyond, the radically other, the "transcendence" traditionally named "God." In the last chapter, we attended to the Christian claim that God understands our need for a spirituality shaped to our humanity. God has indeed spoken concretely into time and space in the life of Jesus of Nazareth. In him we "know" God or at least what truth of God our mortality might bear. But we long not only to know about God, we long to experience the reality of God ourselves—personally in our present time and space, at my kitchen table, today.

The Gospel of John devotes an extraordinary number of pages to the last evening of Jesus' life. He is with his disciples, who are only dimly aware of the portent of this night. Behind these chapters, 13 to 17, lurks one obvious and haunting question. Jesus speaks to it, even if the disciples are afraid to ask it in so many words: "What about after I am gone?" Most all historical movements, including the great religions, have had founders. In every movement this same question inevitably arises: "What becomes of our movement after the founder is gone?" The general answer is usually, "We will remember what the founder said. If he did not do so himself, we'll write his message down in a book and then we will carry on just like he taught us." This has been the experience of historical movements as diverse as Islam and Marxism.

But on that last night around the table this is not what Jesus tells his followers to do after he is gone. In the middle of this long discourse, he says to them, "I have said these things to you while I am still with you. But the Advocate, the Holy Spirit, whom the Father will send in my name, will teach you everything, and remind you of all that I have said to you" (John 14:25–26). Jesus does not charge his followers simply to remember and carry on. Rather, he promises that he will be with them. He will be with them through what Christians have come to call "Holy Spirit."

Our English word *spirit* fails to carry the rich images that it bore in the language of Jesus and in the Greek of the New Testament. The Aramaic word Jesus would have used and the Greek word John uses as he tells the story meant both "wind" and "breath." Our term "Holy Spirit" has come to be covered with a sweet frosting of sentimental religiosity. "Wind" and "breath" were earthy, image-powered words in a way that "spirit" no longer is. We often talk of events and even other people as "having no spirit," a cliché that carries some heft. But how much more evocative it would be to say that they are "out of breath" or that "the wind has been knocked out of them."

I had a class in seminary arcanely named "The Third Article," a title that referred to the third article or section of the Apostles' Creed, which speaks of the Holy Spirit. The professor was a lanky old Scot named Hendry who, in order to make the doctrine relevant to a roomful of twenty-somethings in the mid-1970s, referred to the Holy Spirit in what was doubtless to him the most unconventional of terms. He called the Holy Spirit "the Present Tense of God." Jesus is God "enfleshed," God's gracious answer to our longing to know in terms we can apprehend. The Spirit is God's gracious answer to our longing to experience the reality of God in our present time-and-space-bound life.

But it is not just experience of God that the Spirit bears. The Spirit also teaches by experience and helps us to know who God is in a deeper way. For instance, it would be quite possible to be a world-class expert on Jesus, to know the Gospels from one end to the other, but to keep that knowledge at arm's length, spiritually speaking. It would be possible to affirm that Jesus was a teacher of great historical interest, even unique profundity, but to relegate him to the past, to shut him up in a book, to understand him as nothing more than the "founder." It is the Holy Spirit who bears a living Jesus to us. The Spirit raises him from dead historical memory and makes him alive to us now. In and through the workings of the Spirit, Jesus comes to be for us not only a past reality but a present reality. By this power that the faith has named Holy Spirit, Jesus is not just the memory of a person who once spoke truth but is a living and present Truth.

Several weeks after Jesus' death and resurrection, his followers gathered quietly for a meeting in Jerusalem. The specific occasion was the old Jewish holiday of Pentecost. Perhaps it was a reunion of sorts. They were doubtless still afraid of the local authorities, and it was obviously unclear to them what was to come next. If there was an agenda, it might well have been twofold: remembering the good old days and wrestling with the question, "How do we carry on?" You can imagine them afraid of their shadows after what had happened. Already memories were weakening, and they found themselves picking over the nits of the past. But into what promised to be a sentimental reunion or a depressing committee meeting something they later named "Spirit" exploded uninvited. Pentecost was clearly an event that lay on the other side of easy description. The book of Acts relates the story in terms of wind, fire, a babble of language, and disciples who seemed drunk as skunks in the middle of the morning.

Suddenly, the same Peter who had three times denied even knowing Jesus was on his feet quoting the Old Testament book of Joel: "I will pour out my Spirit upon all flesh." In the next chapter, the same Peter and John who had been in hiding for weeks were not only preaching to the choir of faithful followers but recklessly telling the story of Jesus in the streets of the same town that had executed him a month and a half earlier. The two of them were dragged into court, where they preached a mince-no-words sermon, declaring that they simply must speak; nothing would stop them. By such a Spirit, the story of Jesus Christ burst upon the world, and against all odds the message of a crucified peasant teacher from a remote corner of the Mediterranean conquered one heart after another—Jewish hearts, Greek hearts, Roman hearts, the hearts of slaves and nobility alike. The message was radical and demanding, at sharp odds with the prevailing worldview, and as unlikely a candidate for success as was Jesus himself.

G. K. Chesterton once quipped that the world is divided into two kinds of people: those who see trees waving wildly in the wind and say that the movement of the trees is making the wind, and those who see the same sight and say that the wind is moving the trees. In our present skeptical world, a lot of people declare the former: that the trees are making the wind. People of faith, they hint, are causing Spirit by their moving. Christians are people who insist that spiritually speaking, it is the wind that moves the trees.

Let me shift metaphors and imagine the power of the Spirit in another way. In the summer I sail on Lake Michigan, a body of water that is seldom calm in July and August, at least not along the lee shore between Big and Little Points Sable. But on those rare flat days, the big lake can be like a mirror eighty miles wide. And every once and again on such a summer day, a series of great waves will appear out of nowhere, a huge V-cut in the water slicing across the lake. They are, of course, the wake of some good-sized ship. Our little boat rocks, the halyards slap against the mast, the sails flap, and everyone grabs the coaming to steady themselves. The odd thing is this: Very often the ship that made the wake is nowhere to be seen. Perhaps it is already around Big Point Sable or lost in the summer haze. You never actually saw it with your eyes, but you know it passed by. There is really no other explanation. You also know—even though you never saw it—that it had to have been a vessel of immense power to trail such a wake.

We mortals never "see" God in the literal sense of that verb, but again and again we sense the passing presence of God in the movement that God's unseen Spirit stirs in the world. The Bible is full of the stories of such indirect sightings. The Spirit of God moves over the waters as it did at creation or through a stuffy room as it did at Pentecost, and it troubles things into movement. In our lives, we find our little boat moving suddenly at the power of a great unseen passing vessel. Sometimes our lives pitch violently as this power passes. Often, we have to grab the coaming and hold on for dear life.

Such experiences of the Spirit of God need not be in the form of what we would name "miraculous." Pentecost experiences need not be "Pentecostal" in the current denominational sense of the word. God may and often does choose to work through the Spirit subtly, hidden in routine, veiled in the mundane, camouflaged as coincidence. We recognize the work of the Spirit, not necessarily because some wonder has bedazzled us but because something has come to pass that cannot be credited to human effort alone. Something has moved us; we did not perhaps see it pass, but we know it's there. There is no other explanation.

The Spirit is not only present tense but present power. If we are at all honest with ourselves, we understand that we and this world of ours stand in need of that power which is greater than mortal effort, whether individual or collective. At our most candid we know that we can never love well enough, never work hard enough, never be clever enough, never pray earnestly enough. But our world promulgates a simple and troubling myth of willpower. It tells us that if only we try harder, work harder, pray harder, believe harder, we *can* do it, *we* can do it. Of course, it is true that effort will often bring us closer to most marks, but our every effort is forever bound by our imperfect humanity.

I write these pages not long after the death of Charles Schulz, whose *Peanuts* cartoons often spoke spiritual truth. I recall one in which Linus, who has been chomping on a peanut-butter-and-jelly sandwich, stops to observe his hands. He says to Lucy, "Hands are fascinating things! I like my hands. . . . I think I have nice hands. My hands seem to have a lot of character." Waxing eloquently, he goes on, "These are hands which may someday accomplish great things. . . . These are hands which may someday do marvelous works! They may build mighty bridges or heal the sick, or hit home runs, or write soul-stirring novels! These are hands," he cries out to Lucy, "which may someday change the course of destiny!" Lucy looks at Linus's hands and says, "They've got jelly on them!"

The hard truth is that every human effort has jelly on its hands. Every effort to love falls a little short; our noblest plans have the seeds of failure in the flower. Our resolve, however great, is less than perfectly resolute. We fight a war for peace and find ourselves embroiled in another war. Our plans for social betterment make some things better and some things worse. We finally buy the house we dreamed of and are not much happier after all. We succeed only to find that others have succeeded even more successfully. If we are honest with ourselves, we know that we stand in need of power beyond our power, resolve above our resolve, will beyond our will, love higher than our love.

An English fairy tale tells of a giant and a little tailor (tailors often stand for weakness in fairy tales) who are forced into a contest to determine who is the more powerful. The giant is extraordinarily strong and has been practicing for weeks. He's sure he can beat any other contender. He steps to the line and with every ounce of power in his muscular body throws a stone into the air in a prodigiously high arch. It soars nearly out of sight and finally comes to the ground at a great distance with a thud that nobody can even hear, so far off has it landed. Then the tailor steps to the line, a frail little man with no expression on his face. He lifts his hands into the air and releases a little bird that flies away into the sky, higher and higher, much higher and much farther than any giant might throw any stone.

Several years ago I sat in a hospital waiting room with a frightened family from my congregation. We waited in an anxious silence for a second report from another examining physician. He would suggest a course of treatment, one that would almost certainly include high-risk surgery. A vivacious wife and mother had fallen in her kitchen while cleaning the light fixture that hung from the ceiling. She had somehow landed headfirst and broken her neck. The family had called a specialist and friend who was in Montreal leading an international meeting of neurosurgeons. He got on the next flight back to Ann Arbor. It was he who was doing that second evaluation. He returned to the waiting room and confirmed the grim diagnosis. He then pulled me aside to tell me that the injury was exceptionally serious. In fact, he noted, injuries of this type rarely come into the hospital on their own power. The man is a brilliant and confident young surgeon, straightforward, even brusque in his manner. He is also a good friend and a member of my congregation. He left to scrub for surgery after I told him that I would go pray with the family. Oddly, he returned to the waiting room, striding in as assuredly as usual, and motioned me to follow him into the hallway. "I know you've prayed with the family." He hesitated, looked away and then back at me. Then he asked, "Would you pray with me?"

The Spirit is no substitute for expertise. The Spirit does not replace discipline. We still need to will love and to make choices. We do these things as best we might while at the same time opening ourselves to the Wind of God, turning to Spirit, confessing that we need something more than "us" breathed into our best efforts. Every Sunday before I lead worship, before I preach the sermon I've worked hard to make the best I can, I open an oak door in my study behind which my pulpit robe hangs. On the back of the door, where I cannot miss it, is an old poster with a picture of a small boat under sail, the lone skipper hiking over the side, one hand on the tiller and the other holding the mainsheet. Superimposed over the photo are these words, words I cannot help but see as I reach for my robe. They are words I need to hear before I try hard to do anything: "Free will is like the sailor adjusting the tiller and the sheet. Though it is sometimes a struggle, we can choose to hold the boat of our life steady into the wind of the Spirit. Then our efforts are supported and directed by grace. One caution: Once we have opened souls to such a Wind, we need to be prepared to go where the Spirit blows."

PART III
Life on the Road

Chapter 9

The Geography of God

*I*n part 2, we sneaked up on the Trinity, that most daunting of Christian doctrines and one widely misunderstood today. Many suspect it to be the idle metaphysical speculation of dreamy theologians with too much time on their hands, but in truth, the Trinity is simply the theological result of the church taking the Bible seriously and thinking long and hard about God. In chapter 6, we began with God the Father, the transcendent Other after whom human beings have forever thirsted. In chapter 7, God the Son presents a "specific spirituality" that shapes Divinity into a form we can "see" with mortal eyes, a Person we can know, and a Word we can hear. In chapter 8, we traced the work of God the Holy Spirit as divine reality in the present tense. This third Person of the Trinity is the assurance that God is not just a presence in history but is present with us here and now. The God whom we comprehend in this three-step movement is not so much a God who shows the way; rather, this God is for us the Way. In this third part, we will trace the shape of life along this road.

I mentioned earlier that faith is a two-sided coin—*belief about* God on one side and *trust in* God on the other. I offered fair warning that the trust side of the coin implies that we must take to the road without knowing exactly where it may lead. Nevertheless, it's natural to insist, "If I go, I would like to know at least this: Where is this road going to take me? Does a spiritual road lead me *out* of the world?"

Much of Christian piety over the years, even today, has presented faith as an escape route out of life and its troubles. This road leads "up" to a God imagined to be above the tiresome realities of real day-to-day life. Popular images have pictured a "road to heaven," an afterworld reward or an aloof detachment from this world we but pass through.

The Bible, however, is an insistently earthy collection of books. The "way" it describes does not so much lead out of the world as it leads deeper into and straight through this world. The shape of the Christian life that we will trace in the pages to come is real life lived in relationship with God and transformed by that relationship. God is not so much the destination at the end of the road as God is the road itself. "I am the way, and the truth, and the life," Jesus said. He didn't say, "I am the exit." This way is the entrance into life itself, the fullness of life. These days he might have said, "I am the entrance ramp."

The Trinity that I have described in these last pages portrays God in a radically different way from the God so many people carry around in their heads—that of a remote, uninvolved, and unknowable Deity. The story of God in the Bible is of a Being passionate and tireless in pursuit of relationship: a Creator who enters history to speak to Israel in the drama of the Old Testament, a Redeemer who speaks to us in Jesus Christ, a Sustainer who is present with us in the Spirit. This God is inclined toward us, radically disposed toward relationship, and cannot be spoken of except as God "for us." This is a God whose every act is an extension of the Divine Self, a reaching out of the Divine Being toward us in love to be in communion with us. Not only *does* this God love, but this God *is* love. God not only longs for relationship, but this God *is*—in God's very "self," by God's very "nature"— loving relationship. This is perhaps the most transforming affirmation imbedded in the Trinity, the core truth at the heart of that mystery: an understanding of God who *is* love, a God who *is* relationship, a God who *is* communion. That is to say, the ultimate reality of the universe is a relationship of intense love and profound communion. This Way before us leads into participation in the very life of a God who is communion. The way of faith is not just toward God; it is not simply following God; it is not simply walking with God. The road itself is God.

I have a representation of the Trinity just above the computer in my study. It is on a postcard that someone handed me years ago and is quite unlike the images of the Trinity I remember as a child. They were geometrical shapes fashioned into the dark varnished oak of the pulpit and the trim work behind the choir loft of one of the string of

Presbyterian churches in small Minnesota towns my family attended when I was very young. I remember a puzzle-like shape formed in wood: a triangle set into a three-lobed sort of circle, a mechanical looking three-leafed clover. Its message was clear: Three, yet One, an oaken diagram of Divinity.

The image above my computer is a copy of a fourteenth-century painting, a Russian icon by a master of the form named Rublev. It is called "The Holy Trinity," though at its first level, it is supposed to be a picture of the three visitors who call on Abraham and Sarah by the oaks of Mamre in the eighteenth chapter of Genesis. That story is not really about the Trinity, of course. Abraham invites them to eat and take their rest. One moment they seem to be just desert wanderers, then they seem to be angels, then they are God. Because they were three, Christians have sometimes thought of them as the Trinity, though neither Abraham nor Sarah nor the writer of Genesis had such thoughts in mind.

In Rublev's icon they are seated at a table. They are tall and very slender with strangely long arms. They have wings. One is across the table from me, another visitor to each side. There is an empty place at the table on the side closest to me. The table is white, and its clean expanse draws my eye. On the table is a chalice, and in the chalice is a lamb—the Lamb of God, of course. My postcard is so small that the lamb is very hard to see. Oddest of all, however, is the perspective of the painting. It's all wrong. In proper perspective, all the lines of the planes in a picture must meet at vanishing points in back or to the sides. In this picture, however, the vanishing point is where I am sitting. Behind the picture is not a point but infinite space. The world behind the painting is infinitely larger than the world in which I am sitting. It draws me in.

I have learned that iconographers are required to study for years not only painting but theology and spiritual discipline as well before they may make an icon. The icon is not an image of God; as such it would be idolatrous. Rather, an icon is a window into heaven. I like this icon so foreign to my Protestant eyes because it invites me in. Through this window, I am invited into a heavenly place where a table is set. And around that table is the God-Who-Is-Love, a God whose being is no cold granite mystery but a unity somehow in communion, a God whose very being is love. Not only am I invited into the image by the backward perspective that pulls my eye into eternity, but there is an empty place on my side of the table, a place set for me, a place set for me at love's table.

You may ask, "Where is this table? Is it in the world or out of the world?" Or to ask as bluntly as a child might, "Where does God live?"

To respond to this worthy question, I invite you to imagine something that's not precisely true. Imagine that the cosmos has an upstairs and a downstairs. Imagine that the earth where you and I live is downstairs and that God—the "Man Upstairs"—lives, well . . . upstairs. Never mind that God is not a man and that there is no upstairs, cosmologically speaking. The question of the location of God is much more subtle than up and down—just indulge me. So where does God live, upstairs or down? The Bible suggests two answers to this question, each true in its own way.

The Old Testament story of Jacob's ladder graphically illustrates the first answer. As this tale unfolds, Jacob, the rascal second son of Isaac and the darling of his mother, Rebekah, is a young man on the run. With Mom's help he has just snookered his father out of the all-important family blessing. His big brother Esau is breathing fire and young Jacob decides it would be a good idea to make himself scarce for a while. So he's off to visit Uncle Laban and scout out marriage prospects. He stops for the night along the way, sets a rock under his head, and dreams as you might with a rock for a pillow. He dreams of a ladder between "up there" and "down here." He wakes up and says, "This is the place—right here, the very gate of heaven where you can get up to God." He names the place "Beth-El" ("House of God"). Come morning, he builds a makeshift shrine, a holy road sign for the intersection of heaven and earth.

In the vision of this Bible story, God is clearly "up there." In this first answer, "up there" and "down here" rub against each other in some places, at some times, for some people. There are particular moments in life that are exceptional in their accessibility to the Divine. To use Jacob's image, there are "ladders" here and there that permit occasional traffic between God and humanity. Or you might imagine a membrane stretched between heaven and earth. In some places this membrane is thinner, translucent even, allowing you to trace the movements of God.

The second answer to the "Where does God live?" question is suggested by Psalm 139:

> Where can I go from your spirit?
>   Or where can I flee from your presence?
> If I ascend to heaven, you are there;
>   if I make my bed in Sheol, you are there.
> If I take the wings of the morning
>   and settle at the farthest limits of the sea,
> even there your hand shall lead me.

In the psalmist's vision, ladders are set everywhere between heaven and earth. In fact, there are so many ladders that there is not really an "up there" and "down here." The boundaries are erased. Heaven has descended to earth. Earth has risen to heaven. All is collapsed into one God-infused reality. All places and all times are Beth-El.

Christian faith offers a response to the "Where does God live?" question that subtly blends both of these answers. The first of the two answers suggested that God is "up there" (as it were), but that there are ladders now and then, here and there between "up there" and "down here." The second answer suggests the pervasive presence of God with us—always "down here" with us in our place and time. The Christian doctrine of the incarnation is the historic language that frames in mortal words a mystery that is ultimately beyond any words—namely, the mystery that somehow God "came down" and took on flesh (*incarnate* literally means "in the flesh") and was present with us in the life and death of a human being, Jesus of Nazareth. In the incarnation, the "enfleshing" of God in Jesus Christ, the image of God is offered in human form, a "ladder," a life of revelation allowing us to conceive of Divinity in terms our human understanding can bear. The incarnation whispers the answer: that earth, having once been kissed by God, is forever filled with God, charged with the glory of God. This second and equally radical affirmation of incarnation says that all of this old earth, the very materiality of our being, our sagging bodies, the willow trees, Petosky stones, and Manx cats, all of it has been blessed in incarnation. All of it is touched by the holy. The finite eternally bears the print of the Infinite. The temporal is infused with the Eternal. It is as if ladders are pitched everywhere. Martin Luther said that God wears the mask of the ordinary because God's awful naked majesty would blind us. God wears the mask of creation, the mask of our loved ones, the mask of our neighbors. God wears the mask of the routine, the daily, the mundane. No one has said this more eloquently than poet Francis Thompson, who wrote this poem, "In No Strange Land," with Jacob's old ladder set in the heart of his London:

> O world invisible, we view thee,
> O world intangible, we touch thee,
> O world unknowable, we know thee,
> Inapprehensible, we clutch thee!
>
> Does the fish soar to find the ocean,
> The eagle plunge to find the air—
> That we ask the stars in motion
> If they have rumor of thee there?
>
> Not where the wheeling systems darken,
> And our benumbed conceiving soars!—
> The drift of pinions, would we hearken,
> Beats at our own clay-shuttered doors.
>
> The angels keep their ancient places;—
> Turn but a stone and start a wing!
> 'Tis ye, 'tis your estranged faces,
> That miss the many-splendoured thing.
>
> But (when so sad thou canst not sadder)
> Cry,—and upon thy so sore loss
> Shall shine the traffic of Jacob's ladder,
> Pitched betwixt heaven and Charing Cross.
>
> Yes, in the night, my soul, my daughter,
> Cry—clinging heaven by the hems;
> And lo, Christ walking on the water
> Not of Gennesareth, but Thames![1]

The doctrine of the incarnation, set as it is at the center of the gospel, is a declaration that in Jesus Christ, Eternity has entered time, and Transcendence has trespassed space. This intersection between "up there" and "down here" becomes the definitive signpost for the Christian journey. The inescapable implication of incarnation is that God is not so much to be encountered in the remote and the exceptional, in the "up there" or the miraculous. Rather, God is to be intersected in the proximate, that which is at hand and looks at first to be merely ordinary. Theologian Belden Lane put it well: "The one great practical truth of the incarnation is that the ordinary is no longer at all what it appears. Common things, common actions, common relationships are all granted new definition because the holy has once and for all become ordinary in Jesus Christ."[2]

This Way that is Jesus Christ does not lead us out of real life. Rather, it fills this earthly life with transcendence. The Way is not even "spiritual" in the limp and sentimental sense of that word. Jesus Christ passed through life as it really is, rough edges, disappointments, and terrors included. His life cut a trail for us and laid out a path. His cross stands as the low-water mark of life, emblem of life drained empty. His Way leads us through our lives as they are—complicated mixtures of joy and disappointment, strange stews of nobility and pettiness. His Way has dirt under its fingernails. It goes as deep as life goes: through the cramped office where you face awkward moral choices, through your new house with the windows that never worked right, through the bedroom where you make love, past the TV you channel surf when you're bored and alone. The Way walks you through classrooms where ghost-written midterm essays are routine. It is with you at the table where you eat spaghetti with a sulky teenager. The Way is not a way out of this world. In the end, the Way leads us into a life that may please us deeply. But more to the point, it leads into a life that is pleasing to God. In this integrity between a life that is joy to me and pleasing to God, the Way brings us not mere pleasure, but brings us into a joy that lies on the other side of happiness.

"Where does God live?" The God into whose very life we are invited, whose name is love, who is pictured in Trinity as relationship, is not "up there." The God of creation and incarnation is God with us—incarnate in Christ and present to us in the Spirit. Belden Lane goes on to say that in order to recognize God hidden in the ordinary, two things are needful: attention and love. The first hint for all who take the road is just this: In order to see the Divine in the earthly, we must pay close attention to what may seem merely routine. And we must look at it with eyes full of love. Look up sometimes, but just as often look down and around, close, in your immediate vicinity. Watch faces at the dinner table or at the desk across from you at the office. Look into the movement of the routine that weaves a life; look there for the movement of God. Look at the shapes of trees and noses. Look there for the shape of God. But remember, if you are to see much of anything, you must look with attention and love.

Most of us usually trip through this world blind to the abundance of entirely gratuitous wonder that surrounds us. Such familiarity may not breed contempt, but it tends to breed blindness of the heart.

As a minister, I am occasionally invited to offer what is usually labeled "the invocation" at assorted community events. I accept these invitations most of the time, but if I'm in a frisky mood, I preface my "yes" with a picky little aside about that word "invocation." I just may say, "I'd love to offer an opening prayer, but I don't do invocations." That usually elicits silence from the other end of the phone line. Sometimes the more curious will pursue the matter. "Why not invocations?" This offers me my in. "Because," I answer, "from what little I know about God, God cannot much be invoked. Certainly no words I might mumble could ever invoke the presence of the eternal God. But don't worry, God will be at the meeting no matter what. I'll be glad to pray. But if it's all right, I'll just pray that we might somehow see the Holy Presence that will be there, invocation or no."

Chapter 10

Devotions

Anything that matters demands attention. Anything that matters ultimately demands ultimate attention—devotion. "Devotions" was the word for the Bible reading and prayer that ended the day at Camp Westminster, where I spent several preadolescent summers. We campers sat on our bunks in the cabin while our counselor read a few verses of Scripture and asked us if there was anything anybody wanted to talk about. We looked at the floor and then he mumbled an awkward prayer. His "Amen" and "Lights out!" ended the day. The word "devotions" has fallen out of vogue, perhaps because what it named often seemed just pious punctuation to the real business. But because of its roots I still like it. I like the weight implied in the verb *devote*. If something matters, you devote yourself to it.

From the very beginning, Christians have kept to the Way and been strengthened for the journey by deliberately focusing on God in a variety of regular and disciplined practices. People talk about "practicing Christians" as opposed to people who are Christians in name only. "Practicing" is an odd usage, but I like the implications of this word too. To practice something means you keep at it day after day—you devote yourself to it because you care about it. It also implies that if you're still practicing, you must not be perfect at it yet, which is also true. Practice as they might, practicing Christians never manage perfect performances. But they often show improvement.

In these next chapters, I will focus on three forms of devotion that are at the heart of Christian practice: worship, Bible reading, and prayer. The three of them intersect and overlap, of course. Worship almost always includes reading from the Bible and prayer. Many people pray before or after they read Scripture, whether alone or in a small group. And many people find their way into prayer by reading a passage from the Bible first. Each of the three practices can be either corporate or individual. By separating them, I do not want to give the impression that these three disciplines are entirely separate from each other. Not only do they flow into one another, but in time and with practice, they flow into all of life. As they seep into our larger life, they blur that false and pernicious distinction between "spiritual life" and "real life." In time and with practice, Sunday spills over into Monday. In fact, if it doesn't, you might as well stay home Sunday morning and read the paper.

But before we turn to each of these devotions, I want to respond preemptively to an objection that I hear often enough to expect it now. Practices—anything you do over and over again—whether going to church on Sunday or praying before meals, can be dulled by repetition. When people make this protest, they usually invoke a word that has grown pejorative horns, a verbal slam so hard that the very use of the word sews up the case in their minds. "It's just a *ritual*," they declare, or worse yet, *"dead ritual."* With that label they imagine they have consigned anything religious that one does regularly to the Pleistocene Era. They have a point, of course, but only a point. Prayer and worship, even Bible reading, can indeed be dulled by repetition, but they don't have to be.

The church's love of tradition is an affection that can easily slide into affliction. A century after the Reformation, a certain Reformed congregation in Holland worshiped in a pre-Reformation building. Worshipers leaving the thoroughly Protestant worship service in this building would invariably bow to a white wall at the back of the church. They did this routinely, out of habit passed down from generation to generation. One day it was discovered that beneath the blank wall there was a painting of the Virgin Mary. The iconoclastic Reformers had painted it over a hundred years earlier, but the tradition of venerating it remained, even though no one in the congregation knew it was there or why it was traditional to bow to a blank wall.

Practices grow empty only if you permit them to. The possibility that unexamined repetition may blunt the sharp edge of good tradition should not lead us to jettison every spiritual practice that involves repetition, predictability, or memorization. As the "ritual critique" has edged into fashion, the church's desperate temptation has been to reinvent everything and then reinvent it again and again. Worship has to be new and improved every week. You must devise ever new ways to pray. Churches feel compelled to invent some clever new Bible study technique every year. Why would you memorize anything when you can just read it? The implication of the ritual critique is that if words have been said once, they are exhausted.

But the deeper truth is that human beings crave *both* tradition and innovation. I would offer several reasons for the critical importance of what I stubbornly call ritual. First, in a world where the ground is always shifting, we long for the assurance born by repeated words and actions. Eternal newness gnaws at the few roots still holding us steady. Children hardly ever tire of hearing a good story over and over again. And there is that layer in the adult soul that finds not only comfort but joy and strength in "practicing" the same words and movements time and again. Second, repetition drills it in. I speak at least for myself when I say that I often don't get it the first time. I sometimes don't get it the second or the third time. In fact, I find that I tend to "get it" more and more deeply every time I pray the same words or sing the same hymn. A final argument for ritual remembers that doing things over again blesses our lives with a sacred continuity with those who have gone down this road before us. When I say the Lord's Prayer, I cannot but rejoice that these are words the faithful have been saying for two thousand years. When a congregation says, "We lift them up to the Lord" in response to the invitation, "Lift up your hearts," I imagine all the hearts lifted up these many centuries. Their ancient voices blend with our modern voices as we form the words.

Clearly, some moderation is the rule: Both the old and the new are needful. There is a delicate balance to be found between innovation and tradition. And the balance is at different points on the scale for different Christians; some lean toward tradition, some toward innovation. Innovators need to remember that the fresh becomes tradition in no time. Traditionalists need to remember that tradition has always been a moving, not a static, reality. From experience, I know that saying it over again and hearing it over again carves a groove in my soul. And I know that when the hard times come, that very groove may be God's way in and my way through.

Chapter 11

Worship: Turning to the Center

Don McCullough begins his book *The Trivialization of God* with this observation about modern worship:

> Visit a church on a Sunday morning—almost any will do—and you will likely find a congregation comfortably relating to a Deity who fits nicely within precise doctrinal positions, or who lends almighty support to social crusades, or who conforms to individual spiritual experiences. But you will not likely find much awe or a sense of mystery. The only sweaty palms will be those of the preacher unsure whether the sermon will go over; the only shaking knees will be those of the soloist about to sing the offertory.[1]

Annie Dillard has been quoted again and again on this same point, usually from this passage in *Teaching a Stone to Talk*:

> Why do people in churches seem like cheerful, brainless tourists on a packaged tour of the Absolute? ... On the whole, I do not find Christians, outside of the catacombs, sufficiently sensible of conditions. Does anyone have the foggiest idea what sort of power we so blithely invoke? ... It is madness to wear ladies' straw hats and velvet hats to church; we should all be wearing crash helmets. Ushers should issue life preservers and signal flares; they should lash us to our pews. For the sleeping god may wake someday and take offense, or the waking god may draw us out to where we can never return.[2]

People often seem to imagine that worship is either entertainment, therapy, or education, perhaps some blending of the three. If it's entertainment, worship would seek to please us in some way, distracting us from routine and invoking happy feelings. This view would suggest that the worship hour should attempt to be as engaging as the flood of entertainment that pours into our secular experience. There may indeed be some sense in which worship entertains, but such a concept is far too trivial.

The language of therapy has become universal in our age. This vocabulary evaluates experiences in terms of whether or not they promote psychological or spiritual healing. If it is therapy, worship is judged by the extent to which it makes one "feel better" or brings "healing" into a person's life. There is, of course, a sense in which worship must do just that, but to understand it so simply reduces the worship of God to something much smaller.

Finally, among many Protestants, worship long ago started to look a lot like school. Worship was approached as an opportunity for the spiritual and intellectual improvement of Christians, largely through instructive sermons. Of course, Christian worship ought to teach. In worship, a congregation learns the things of Christ. But again, this category is simply too small to comprehend the fullness of worship.

The insufficiency of each of these categories lies in the fact that they are facing the wrong direction. Each is oriented toward entertaining, healing, or educating *the worshiper*. But the spiritual vector of worship ought to be in exactly the opposite direction—toward God.

Here is the heart of the matter. Worship doesn't really have a "purpose" in the utilitarian sense of these three categories. Maybe worship is just a glorious and transforming waste of time. At its most profound, worship is nothing but a deliberate and repeated activity in which we are called to turn away from self and turn toward God. As such, it is "devotional" in the best sense of that crusty old word. Worship is nothing less than an attempt to set the order of creation aright. The creature owns her creaturehood. Honest confession is spoken. Praise is offered. The worshiper surrenders his pretense to be a god; all turn in adoration to the One who *is* God. In this dramatic enactment of the fundamental "rightness" of things lies transformation and restoration. Life edges into proper balance. We are free to be who we are—no more but no less. We discover the liberation that comes with being forgiven and accepted by both God and neighbor. We are freed from the pretense of autonomy and invulnerability. We no longer imagine that we have to be in control of everything. Worship is no less than weekly practice at not being God.

Through the ages and around the globe, Christians have always worshiped in a dizzying and dazzling variety of ways. The stark and spontaneous minimalism of a Quaker prayer service—white paint and a few lean words—is in utter contrast to the Russian Orthodox liturgy: a sea of icons, the ancient complexity of the prayers, and the eye-popping vestments of the priests. It is impossible to generalize about the content and shape of all Christian worship; nevertheless, most traditions most of the time have included several common elements.

For instance, with few exceptions, Christians worship on Sunday, the day of the resurrection, the day that remembers and celebrates that core affirmation of the triumph of life over death. Christian worship almost always includes prayer. Some churches favor prayers from books, words carved lovely by the ages. Others pray as the Spirit moves. Christian worship almost always includes, in fact is often centered on, the reading of passages from the Bible. Some churches read the Bible according to lectionaries, set patterns of readings for each Sunday. Others prefer to select readings according to the issues of the day. In most churches, the reading of the Bible is followed by an explanation of the meaning of the Scripture that was read, a presentation variously called a meditation, sermon, or homily. Nearly all Christian traditions incorporate music, especially sung music, in worship. Most traditions also include an opportunity for worshipers to respond to God by offering something of themselves. This can include a collection of money for the support and work of the church or a rededication of worshipers to the faith by saying a creed.

Most Christian worship also incorporates sacraments, symbolic enactments or ritual dramas, if you will. Different traditions count different sacraments, but the two that are almost universally kept are baptism and Holy Communion, also called the Lord's Supper, Eucharist, or Mass. Baptism, as we saw earlier in this book, is the sacred act marking the beginning of the Christian journey. Baptism initiates or adopts a child or adult into the family of faith and occurs but once in life. Its governing symbol is water, of course. That water, running down the forehead of a child or through the hair of an adult, evokes images of the life-giving power of God, for little on this earth lives without water. Water also bespeaks transition and commitment. Water usually appears in the biblical story at points of decision or commitment: Noah's flood that starts everything over, the children of

Israel crossing the River Jordan into the promised land to begin again, Jesus' baptism in that same water marking the beginning of his work.

Though different Christian traditions understand the details differently, in every church the signs of bread and wine govern the sacrament of Holy Communion. Bread and wine recall Jesus' last supper with his disciples and evoke memories of that night: love, betrayal, and subsequent sacrifice. But it is more than remembering. For most Christians the sacrament is a sign of the living presence of Christ with us. Holy Communion in most churches is not just a memorial meal but also a banquet celebrating life with God and life in community. Just as real food nourishes our bodies, the spiritual food of Holy Communion is a sign of the way God's living presence nourishes our souls.

"What did you get out of that service?" is a question asked on the way to brunch on many a Sunday morning. There is nothing wrong with critiquing worship, but this is the wrong question because it again aims the vector of worship straight at us. It assumes that worship is another form of entertainment, educational opportunity, or therapeutic session. The better question might be: What did you lose in that service? What burden did you drop at the foot of the cross? What pride did you shed? What gnawing anger are you going home without? What lie do you no longer believe?

We tend to carry a critical demeanor into church, as if worship were a performance, with the minister and the choir as actors on a stage and all of it a deliberate production aimed to please, improve, or educate. A hundred and fifty years ago, Søren Kierkegaard observed that we suffer from role confusion in worship. We understand the congregation as an audience, the minister as a performer, and God as the prompter. Sticking with the stage metaphor, he said we need to flip this on its head: The congregation are the actors, the minister is a prompter, and God is the audience. The opportunity we are met with whenever we darken the Sunday morning door is to give ourselves again to God, to lose ourselves in the Absolute, to turn away from self and re-center on God.

The indirect result of this reordering of the moral universe, its by-product if you will, is the nurturing of the worshiper toward integrity, wisdom, and joy. This integrity is more than mental health. This wisdom is more than education. And this joy is so much more than entertainment. But if worship pursues any of these goals *directly*, it will miss the mark, if only because it is headed 180 degrees in the wrong direction. If you and I enter worship facing anywhere but toward God, the experience may please us, it may inform us, it may comfort us, but it will hardly *transform* us.

At the heart of the ancient Temple in Jerusalem was a room called the Holy of Holies. It was so sacred that only one person, the high priest, could go into it, and he but once a year, on the Day of Atonement. The room was empty except for a single throne, which was itself empty. Two gold cherubim spread their wings above it, facing each other over the place where nothing was. When the high priest entered the Holy of Holies, he had to do but one thing. He had prepared to do it for months. He was to utter the ineffable name of God, a name made up of four letters of the Hebrew alphabet, a name so holy that no one really knew how to pronounce it because ordinarily no one dared say it. Even the meaning of the name was wrapped in mystery. Maybe it meant "I am who I am." It was often said that it was simply the sound of breathing, so when the high priest went into the Holy of Holies on that one day, all he really had to do was breathe. Tradition adds this savory detail: Before the high priest went into the Holy of Holies, other priests tied a rope around his leg. In case he was struck down in the presence of God, they would have a way to drag him out without risk to themselves.

That image stands in delicious contrast to the easy worship— "comfortable and accessible"—that so many people seem to think the world wants. If we seek comfort, it is there, but it usually lies on the other side of self-abandoning praise, intense prayer, and honest confession. If we seek an "accessible" wisdom, it too is there, but such wisdom comes by thinking hard. Worship that poses no risk is something else. Worship that does not make you anxious once and again, worship that fails to stretch your mind and spirit to the edge of discomfort, is something less than worship. If worship is no more, ask this question: In what direction are you facing?

Chapter 12

Packing a Bible

*T*hat great nineteenth-century preacher Charles Spurgeon is reported to have said, "The way you defend the Bible is the same way you defend a lion. You just let it loose." The books of the Bible range in age from about two to three millennia, yet these ancient words still have a power to capture spiritual imaginations and change lives. But the book only has such power if you open it and turn it loose. A great many Bibles, even those kept by the faithful, show little wear. They decorate bookshelves and nightstands, with birth announcements and marriage licenses tucked in their onionskin pages, where they run no risk of getting lost.

My guess is that Christians have Bibles in excellent condition for two reasons: First, they are nervous about what they will encounter if they actually read the book. They know just enough about the contents from Sunday school and sermons to know that it's not your typical self-help book. They guess rightly that reading it will be demanding. Not only will the act of reading itself be demanding, but the content will doubtless make demands on their lives. There are, they might recall, all those Old Testament prophets with their uncompromising words about justice and the poor. And there is Jesus, who seems to say so much about turning cheeks, giving coats away, and taking up one's cross.

But I am inclined to guess that the more pervasive reason that Christians leave their Bibles closed is that they have been made to feel that they are not competent to understand what they read. For modern Christians, there is sharp irony in this lack of biblical self-confidence. Throughout the Middle Ages, the church had told the faithful that the Bible was not for them. It was generally not available in the languages of the common people, only in the Latin of the church. "But don't worry; we will interpret it to you" was the overt message. The implication was that even if they could read, putting a Bible in the hands of common people could be dangerous.

One of the goals of the Protestant Reformation was to translate the Bible into the language of the people, teach them to read, and then make the Scriptures widely available (the printing press had just been invented). This grand cultural and spiritual project was stunningly successful. Many average churchgoers, not just the clergy, knew the content of the Bible so well that poets and novelists in the following centuries could include subtle Scripture references, trusting that their readers would catch them.

The Bible is still the best-selling book in the world. So why are so many sold and never read? It's not only that people are right when they guess that what they might encounter in it will make demands; it's something more. Over the last century and a half, the Bible has been studied using critical academic methodologies in a way that it never was before. These study methods are complex and sophisticated, demanding that scholars devote entire careers to narrow areas of expertise. This kind of Bible study—often called higher criticism—has yielded new and deeper understandings of Scripture. But it has also communicated something damaging to the 99 percent of Christians who are not biblical scholars. Like most moderns, they respect expertise, and the very existence of this kind of biblical specialization has suggested that if you are not a scholar, you could hardly be expected to grasp the labyrinthine complexities to which scholars devote lifetimes.

The core affirmation that Jews and Christians have made about Scripture is that it is "God's word." In the past and even today, some have understood this to mean that God dictated the words verbatim and that the biblical writers merely copied them down. But most Christians and Jews have come to understand their respective Scriptures as being a rich mingling of divine and human speech. In short, inspiration does not mean divine dictation. Rather, the Spirit worked in and through human writers to create a written witness that is a subtle intertwining of heaven and earth. The great debate of the last several centuries of academic study of the Bible has been over precisely what in the Bible is human and what is divine.

Some Christians have made a key distinction about how the Bible is the word of God by making a point of not capitalizing the word *word* when it refers to Scripture. The reasoning goes like this: Christians (and most Jews for that matter) believe that God has made God's Self known in history, in revelatory events, in what God has actually done in our down-to-earth human story. In the Old Testament, God acts in history by freeing the ancient people of Israel from Egyptian slavery and giving them land and law. Through that historical narrative, God makes God's Self known as One who values freedom, gives identity, and cares passionately about right and wrong, all fresh ideas some three thousand years ago.

In the New Testament, God's decisive act of self-disclosure is through the life, death, and resurrection of Jesus. In these real-world historical events, God again "speaks," articulating a love for humanity, a passion for mercy, an ethic of welcome, a boundless grace and compassion, a willingness to suffer with us, and then the final word declaring that with God, life trounces death. For Christians, these events themselves, indeed the very person of Jesus Christ, are the divine "Word." As such, when the word *Word* is used to refer to Jesus Christ, it is capitalized. The Bible has authority and is the word (small *w*) of God because it tells the story of the Word (capital *W*) of God. The point is that the Bible's authority is derivative and penultimate, powerful because it points to the events of Jesus' life, death, and resurrection, the Word in the ultimate and capitalized sense. The Bible itself is not precisely the revelation of God, rather it is the written witness to the revelatory things that God has done.

Modern readers misunderstand and misrepresent the Bible, when they read it as if it were a book of twenty-first-century science or a volume of history written within the strictures of the latest historiography. To set the Bible up against evolutionary theory, for instance, or to read it as if it were a modern objective history of the ancient Middle East effectively demeans Scripture. Such an approach reduces the Bible to just another source of authority on a par with others. But Scripture was not written to detail the process by which God created the cosmos. It was not written as ancient political history. Rather the Bible bears true and faithful witness to spiritual truth, the truth about God and God's relationship to humanity.

The Bible is not a single book, but a collection of sixty-six books, a wildly diverse spiritual library written over a period of perhaps a thousand years. Rather than imagining the Bible as if it were a tome dropped from the heavens, imagine the Bible as a great conversation of people who have witnessed what God has done in history. Imagine these eyewitnesses gathered around a big round table. They certainly don't see everything just the same. They converse and even argue with each other, they agree with each other and sometimes disagree. And they quote each other all the time.

In the same way, the books of the Bible don't all see God in exactly the same way. One book often agrees with another, one sees things from one vantage point, another from a different point of view. One book sometimes argues with another. They quote each other all the time. It's lively conversation. Now, staying with this picture of a great conversation of witnesses gathered at a big round table, when we read the Bible, it's as if we're pulling up our chair to listen in and to put in our two cents' worth. We hear the agreements and disagreements; we listen to strident voices and irenic voices. If we were to listen to just one voice, the story would be incomplete, just as reading one book of the Bible is not the whole story. To study the Bible is to join the conversation. We bring our witness, our experience, and our point of view to the table. As we listen, resonate, and even argue, the ancient words come home to our time and place. They invade our lives and, by the Spirit, come alive to us.

In many congregations church members read the Bible on Sunday mornings. Often their reading is profoundly moving. Some lay readers have squeaky voices and pronounce "Caesarea Philippi" in innovative ways, but it seems crucial that the minister not do the reading. When church members read, it makes a point nobody has to explain: The Bible belongs to the people, not to the minister and not to the scholars.

Worship in most traditions moves around two centers: the Word and the sacraments. The Word itself moves in two steps, the reading of the Bible and the sermon that follows. The sermon is no mere spiritual essay, much less the pastor's thoughts for the week. It is an exposition of Scripture read, an attempt to interpret and apply to a specific time and place the biblical texts of the day. It is a daunting task, one that honest preachers approach with fear and trembling. Again, it is the Holy Spirit that bears these frail, mortal, sometimes foolish words to the listening ears of the congregation and makes them live.

The nature of the Bible's authority is such a subtle and complex question that it has unhappily left many Christians in the pews with the impression that it is all just too complicated for mere laypeople. In many Christian traditions, a "prayer for illumination" is offered before or after the Bible is read in Sunday worship. This is no mere pious gesture but an acknowledgment that both preacher and congregation stand in need of the Spirit in order to preach about and understand what is read. The prayer for illumination is tacit confession that the Bible is not finally brought home to us by cleverness, scholarship, or even human insight. Rather, the Spirit works in these ancient words to apply them to our lives in the same way that the Spirit worked in the ancient writers to make their mortal words more than cleverness, scholarship, or insight. This same discipline of prayer commends itself to personal or small-group reading of the Bible. Prayer for illumination asks that God's light shine on the page and confesses our need for a wisdom above our own.

Several years ago, a controversial group of radical biblical scholars called the Jesus Seminar captured media attention by publishing versions of the Gospels in which they labeled words ascribed to Jesus in four different ways. In their scheme, red meant that most of the group thought Jesus actually did say the words, pink meant that most thought Jesus said something similar, gray meant that most thought Jesus did not say those words but that they may express a genuine idea of Jesus, and black meant that most of the seminar didn't believe that Jesus actually said them. Even more sensational was the manner of determining group consensus. The seminar voted with colored beads much like a college fraternity might vote on new members. These scholars have garnered much of the attention they sought and have been both praised and vilified. After learning of this system, James Sanders, one of the great Bible scholars of our time, said, "There is really only one question: 'Did they pray before voting?'" (They did not.) The point is this: scholarship matters. It can be an essential aid to our understanding of Scripture. The Bible demands hard thinking of us and we owe it to ourselves to be informed readers. But important as scholarship is, it is even more essential to read prayerfully and expectantly.

The Bible is not a puzzle. The unintentional message that such academic work has given to many readers is that the truth of Scripture is hidden in some kind of conundrum. Bible reading becomes puzzle solving. "What does such and such stand for?" becomes the definitive question. Indeed, some of the writers of the Bible made rich use of symbols. Words and images served as shorthand for illusive or complicated ideas. Although some are inscrutable even to the scholars, most biblical symbols are reasonably clear. The Bible is simply not a book of secret writing.

Neither is the Bible essentially a book of advice or a collection of rules. This is a disappointment to readers who approach the Bible from their experience with self-help literature. There is indeed good counsel in its pages and there are laws, but 80 percent of the Bible is narrative. It is mostly the story of things that happened. In and through these things that happened, God speaks. This implies that the reader's job is not to "decode," nor is it to sift words for some kernel of good advice or a rule for living. Rather, we come to these sacred stories in much the way we naturally read any narrative. When you read stories, you usually bring three things to the reading. You hardly have to think about them. Usually you do it automatically.

1. *Identity.* With whom do you identify in the story? When you read any narrative and find yourself deeply engaged, you usually "see yourself" in characters in the story. In this way, the story engages you and begins to work on and in you. If you read Scripture at a distance, as a subject of objective study to be examined distant from you personally, it will have a harder time finding you, though it may anyway. More than one reader has read the Bible as a requirement for a comparative religion class and suddenly found that he or she is grappling not with mere religious ideas but with the living God.

The character with whom you identify in a particular Bible story may change with time and circumstance. Take as an example Jesus' familiar parable of the Prodigal Son. As a rambunctious and candid seventeen-year-old, you might find yourself identifying with the Prodigal. A couple of decades later, you might see yourself reflected in the father. There may be days when you feel like you've gotten the short end of the stick and you can see the older brother's point about fairness. Many, if not most, Bible stories are multilayered, wonderfully variegated, and subtle.

2. *Recognition.* The best stories always elicit the same response. You put the book down on your lap, nod your head knowingly, and say, "Isn't that just the way it is!" This recognition may be so startling that you laugh out loud. This is the "Aha!" response that cries out with the joy of seeing the truth at last. You come to recognize in the story a truth long hidden, often some true thing from your own personal story. Perhaps it was long there and half-known, but you had not seen it so clearly before. In such recognition, the movement of the story and the movement of your life run alongside each other. You see the truest things about yourself in the mirror of what you read, and reflected there you are able to recognize truth formerly hidden in proximity and familiarity. The Bible is revelation not just because it communicates general and abstract truths about God. Revelation worthy of the name is always personal and intimate. The Bible is not so much a book about God in general as it is a book about God and you.

3. *Imagination.* Reading the Bible both requires and creates imagination. The imaginative reader opens herself up to Scripture by daring to identify with characters and by recognizing the way Scripture mirrors the truth about God and his life. By daring to enter into the world of the Bible—its characters, plots, and spiritual viewpoints—one must exercise sacred imagination. Several times in my life, I have read long novels or novel series that have invited me to enter into the world the author has created. I read Patrick O'Brian's epic series of twenty novels set largely on ships of the British navy during the Napoleonic Wars. Halfway through, I started to find that the speech and manners, the assumptions and viewpoints of two hundred years ago started to sound "right" in a way that they had not when I read the first pages. Likewise, in reading Scripture you find yourself drawn imaginatively into what is at first a strange and unfamiliar world. The assumptions of the writers and characters, their viewpoints and cultures, seem strange and foreign. But as your imagination draws you in, the moral shape and spiritual contours of the biblical world begin to look more familiar. This is not to say that the modern reader should adopt the Bible's premodern viewpoints about physics or biology. It is rather that the Bible's theological and spiritual viewpoints come to be like a new pair of prescription eyeglasses. Viewed through these lenses, that which was once fuzzy comes to be seen clearly.

Imagination also implies playfulness. It is not at all irreverent to read the Bible playfully. People often read Scripture ponderously, confusing seriousness with humorlessness. But as the writer Flannery O'Connor once noted, "The maximum amount of seriousness admits the maximum amount of comedy." The Bible has none of the Comedy Channel's easy laughs. But it is brimming with truthful irony and loaded with the kind of surprises that may make you laugh out loud. Reading the Bible is a joy—if you let it be itself. It tickles and goads, spikes and skewers. It makes us weep and then laugh while still drying the tears. It was none other than the very serious father of the church, Augustine, who quipped that "scripture is God's house, and he wants us to play in it."

The Bible serves as a "map" for the God-journey in the sense that it is the definitive travelogue of those who walked the road before us. On their way, they were given to witness events through which God's purposes intersected earthly history. This book of journey stories does not offer short answers to hard questions. Rather, it is the story of those who went before and an invitation to follow them into the heart of the matter. The answers (that is too little a word) are there, but mostly they come to be found along the Way. The Truth (the better word) of Scripture comes in the back-and-forth of lively conversation between my life and the Bible I have packed for the journey.

According to the last chapter of Luke's Gospel, on Easter morning some of the women who had followed Jesus dashed back from the tomb to tell the disciples the good news they had encountered. But "these words seemed to them [the disciples] an idle tale, and they did not believe them." How does Scripture become truth we can trust— or is it another idle tale? You and I, living two thousand years after the fact, are in the same pickle as those eleven apostles who stayed back when the women went to the tomb. The women ran home, bursting into the room with news of what they had seen. The disciples hadn't seen a thing and didn't believe it. All they had was the women's word for it, and it wasn't quite enough.

Like them, we've seen no empty tombs, no angels in dazzling apparel. They had the women's story, we have the story in the Bible, and the question is the same then and now: Is somebody else's word quite enough? Do you and I believe it just because it's in the Bible?

Idle tales abound—just surf the Internet for an hour or read the tabloid headlines in the grocery store checkout line. So here is the Easter question: What brings people to believe these particular words? How is it that Scripture becomes revelation, life-changing truth for you and me all these years later?

Before we approach that question, let's back up for a moment. At the most basic level, there are two ways to know something. First, I can take somebody else's word for it. I can know something because somebody told me even though I haven't seen it for myself. I believe that there is a city in Japan named Tokyo, even though I've never been there. People I trust, people who have no reason to make up stories, have told me about Tokyo and swear it's there. I also believe in the germ theory, even though I have never seen a germ. I believe that the earth goes around the sun, even though it's not immediately obvious. People with microscopes and telescopes say these things are so; it makes sense, so I more or less take their word for it.

But when the women told the eleven disciples back in the city about their experience, the disciples refused to take them at their word. This piece of information was too extraordinary to be credible. You and I are in much the same position when we read the Bible. We were obviously not there in person. There is indeed very good internal evidence for the truth of many of the Gospel's claims: How else to explain the radical transformation that swept over those dispirited disciples? We may trust the people who wrote the remembrances down, but is their say-so alone quite enough? How many people these days can really subscribe to the bumper-sticker philosophy, "The Bible says it. I believe it. That's it"? For better or worse, you and I are back with those eleven disciples and we're looking at the women, looking to the Bible, "I know what you're saying, but I need to experience something for myself. I need some confirmation."

The second basic way to know something is to experience the truth for yourself. Maybe you touch it yourself, smell it, taste it, see it with your own eyes, hear it with your own ears, and—and this is key—know it with your own heart. This is how those skeptical disciples eventually came to trust Easter to be true. Their own experiences confirmed the story. And it is how you and I and millions of skeptics over the ages have confirmed Scripture to be revelation for us. Our experience has vouchsafed the story.

There is more to Luke's Easter story. Those skeptical eleven do come to believe. Two of Jesus' followers leave Jerusalem for a seven-mile walk to a village named Emmaus. On the road, a stranger they do not recognize falls in step with them and together they rehearse the events of the last few days. They talk about life; they talk about faith. They persuade the stranger to stay for dinner when they get to Emmaus. And in the breaking of bread they somehow come to sense Christ alive and present with them. This story is obviously trans-rational. It is not a story about simple seeing with the eyes or simple hearing with the ear. The experience on the road to Emmaus is enig-matic, elusive, and mysterious. It's a story of a firsthand knowing, knowing with the heart.

A few years ago, I came across a story told by Archbishop Iakovos of the Greek Orthodox Church:

> In a large American city, I was engaging in small talk with some families who had gathered in a sitting room. During a lull in the conversation, a three-year-old walked up to me rather boldly and asked, "Can you come with me?" "Yes," I replied. I was rather impressed that this little boy would be bold enough to take the ini-tiative with a strange grown-up—especially one whose face was covered with a white beard and who was dressed in the long black robes and imposing neck cross. . . . But this youngster was com-pletely undaunted. He took my hand and led me to the corner of the room, away from the other guests. Almost before I could bend down to his level, he put his important question to me, "How can I see God?" The archbishop replied simply: "Most often we don't see God on the outside with our eyes. Instead, we see him on the inside, with our hearts."[1]

It's a sweet and naive story. But in its simplicity, it probes the very truth that the French mathematician and philosopher Blaise Pascal was aiming at when he wrote, "Reason's last step is the recognition that there are an infinite number of things which are beyond it."

Discovering that Scripture is indeed revelation is this kind of know-ing. It is experiential, that is, it's not just somebody else saying so. It's a subtle knowing, heartfelt, precisely heartfelt. It's just out of reach of mere seeing with the eye or knowing by reason. It is a way of know-ing that honors the mind; it *is* reasonable, yet deeper and higher than the five senses or reason alone. We are like those first disciples: Somebody else's word is not quite enough. We need to know it for ourselves, but that knowing for ourselves is subrational and suprarational, every bit as mysterious as it was on that walk to Emmaus. Those two who made the walk described it so aptly when they reflected, "Were not our hearts burning within us?"

You and I have seen no empty tombs, no angels in dazzling apparel. Yet, in another way, we have experiences that confirm the deep truth of Scripture to us. We have such experiences along the road of life, hidden among the days, woven into words at table, incarnate in the routine of life. We see for ourselves every time courage unaccountably conquers fear, every time some mortal soul miraculously rises above self, every time life stares down death, when we see hope where there should be no hope, goodness where there should be none. We see it for ourselves in the inexplicable, gratuitous loveliness of creation.

And then, as we look at life through the lens of Scripture, it all makes sense like nothing ever made sense before. Through our own experience, the Bible, this witness of the ages, this narrative of God, this story of death and life, comes to make sense like nothing else because it fills the God-shaped hole in the human heart as though it had been custom-created to fit that space.

Chapter 13

On Your Knees

Like any good pilgrim to the Holy Land, I visited the Western Wall in the Jewish Quarter of Jerusalem. Jews call it the Wailing Wall and go there to lament the destruction of the great Temple. They also come to pray. The Temple was destroyed in AD 70 at the end of the Jewish Wars by Titus, the son of the emperor Vespasian. The wall was not part of the old Temple itself; it is a remnant of a colossal retaining wall that shores up the side of the mount on which the Temple had stood. This is, of course, the same Temple to which Jesus had come to pray, preach, and tip over tables some forty years before its destruction.

I watched men and women praying in the hot sun—separately, of course. Many of the men were wrapped in prayer shawls and rocked back and forth, lost in their prayers. It is also customary to write prayers on slips of paper and tuck them into the cracks between the immense blocks of Herodian stone. To a height of maybe eight feet, the wall is covered with thousands of little white prayers sticking out of the joints. I also noticed several men in black standing near the wall and talking on cell phones. I asked our guide what they were doing. He told me that people call from all over the world and for a small fee these agents write their prayers on slips of paper and put them in the wall. And now, he added, you can do it by e-mail. The agent prints it out and tucks your prayer into the wall that very day. The question this scene asks is one of the foundational religious questions for Jews and Christians, indeed for most religious people: Does prayer work?

There are at least two answers to that question. The first assumes that what is really meant is, "Does prayer lead to the effect I want?" With all my being, I trust that the answer to that question is, "Yes . . .

sometimes." I know that I, for one, pray for things to work out the way I want them to. In a conversation about prayer before dinner with some colleagues not long ago, one of them—a longtime friend and something of a liberal on most matters—set his glass of white wine on the table, looked me in the eyes and said, "Lindvall, I want the truth. Do you pray before airplanes take off?" "Always," I said. "Can't help it." "So do I," he answered. "So do I." Some 90 percent of Americans pray, surveys show. We pray about the test result due from the clinic on Tuesday. We pray before finals. We pray for the homeless and the hungry. We pray when we're depressed and don't know why. And all of us have stories to tell about prayers that come to be answered: inexplicable miracles, healings that set doctors to shaking their heads, coincidences that are just God's way of remaining anonymous. In some way that imagination cannot codify, I trust that God is moved by passionate and compassionate prayers. In a way that I do not pretend to comprehend, sometimes, sometimes the vector of events seems to be bent by prayer, as if by some magnetic force.

Of course, answers do not always come in the way we want them to come. Saint Augustine wrote a disarmingly frank spiritual autobiography, *Confessions,* in which he tells almost all. Augustine grew up in Carthage in North Africa, the son of a devout mother named Monica. Augustine was himself on the edge of faith. Like any bright twenty-something, he wanted to go to Rome. His mother passionately wanted him to stay in Carthage. "Not to Rome," she prayed, "with its paganism and godlessness." One day Augustine deceived his mother by telling her that he wanted to visit a friend aboard a ship in Carthage's harbor. A savvy mom, she offered to go along. Augustine protested that she would hardly want to be exposed to all those coarse longshoremen and that she would do better to take herself to the nearby Chapel of St. Cyprian and pray.

So she did, and while she prayed that her son remain in Carthage, the ship sailed to Rome with Augustine on board—another rebellious son off to the ancient Big Apple. But here is the twist: It was in Rome, with its paganism and godlessness, that Augustine happened to walk by a monastery wall over which he heard the voice of Saint Ambrose reading aloud from the Bible. And it was that hearing of Scripture which set about the events that led to Augustine's conversion to faith. In the denial of his mother's prayer was its answer. Later, Augustine

would himself pray, "But thou in thy hidden wisdom didst give the substance of her desire, yet refused the thing she prayed for." It's an eternal theme; sixteen hundred years later, country singer Garth Brooks would make it big in a hit in which he crooned, "Sometimes I thank God for unanswered prayer."

An old Chinese folktale tells of a farmer who owned only one horse. He depended on the horse to pull the plow and to draw the wagon. One day a bee stung the horse, and in fright it ran away into the mountains. His neighbors said, "We are really sorry about your bad luck in losing your horse." But the old farmer shrugged and said, "Bad luck, good luck—who is to say?" A week later his horse came back accompanied by twelve wild horses, and the farmer was able to corral all the fine animals. News spread, and his neighbors returned and said, "Congratulations on this fine bonanza," to which the old man again shrugged and said, "Good luck, bad luck—who can say?" The farmer's only son decided to make the most of what looked like good fortune and started to break the wild horses so that they could be sold. But he got thrown from one of them and broke his leg. At the news of this accident, his neighbors came again, saying, "We are so sorry about the bad luck of your son's fall." And of course, the old man said, "Bad luck, good luck—who can say?" Several weeks later, war broke out among the provinces of China. The army came through the village and conscripted all the young men, but because the old man's son was so badly injured, he did not have to go.

Time and again, the truth is that it is not God, but I, who must do the bending. The answer that comes is not that God will give me what I want; the answer is for me to change what I want. Remember, any spiritual geography that includes God must place God at the center of the map. In prayer, we reorient ourselves to the center rather than demand the center reorient toward us.

I have a friend, a man of deep faith, who was diagnosed with Parkinson's disease when he was still in his fifties. He is a man who prays. He prayed that he might be healed. But he now has had Parkinson's disease for decades. Yet he once told me that his prayers have been answered. He looked at me and said, "I have been healed, but not of Parkinson's disease; I have been healed of my fear of the disease." Does prayer work? If you mean, "Do you get what you pray

for?" the answer is "Yes, sometimes." Sometimes—for we know that all prayers are not answered as we pray them.

After the Last Supper and just before his arrest, Jesus went to the Garden of Gethsemane on the Mount of Olives. He prayed alone a prayer that is utterly remarkable for at least two reasons: First, the prayer is scandalously honest. The Christ, the Son of God, admits grief and fear and asks that the cup he sees coming—namely, death— be removed from his path. Second, the prayer is utterly remarkable in this context because it is not answered, at least not in the way he prays it. "Remove this cup," he prays, and the next day they pounded nails through the palms of his hands.

So did Jesus' prayer not work? There is a second answer to the "Does prayer work?" question. That answer is deeper and more subtle. Prayer is not simply about changing the course of events. The second answer assumes that prayer is not just about changing the outside world. Prayer is also about changing me and my relationship to God. In prayer, the one who prays edges—prayer by prayer—into a deeper intimacy with God. In prayer, we lay ourselves spiritually bare, just as Christ did. Our words carve a space for a relationship with the One who is beyond us. When I tell God what I presume God must already know, I am build-ing—word by word—a relationship with the Absolute. No part of me is hidden. Pretense is demolished. I am known and I know that I am known. I say the words not just to affect the will of God, but I pray so that I might in conversation press deeper into an intimacy with the Tran-scendent One.

In time, prayer comes to be not so much a way to change things around us as it is a method by which we come into the presence of God. Evelyn Underhill, the British scholar of mysticism and worship, was given to noting that most of us spend our lives as if we were con-jugating three verbs: "to want," "to have," and "to do," though in the end, only the verb "to be" has ultimate significance. Simply "being" in the presence of God is the essence of the spiritual life and the deep-est purpose of prayer.

Prayer is not fundamentally utilitarian. It is not just about chang-ing things. Prayer is not simply a matter of bending the vector of divine will toward my needs and my hopes, not even the loftiest and

most selfless of them. Instead, to pray is to edge into relationship with God. When you do that, it isn't so much God's mind that is changed; rather, your mind—and your heart—are changed. In prayer, the will of the infinite One and your human will come slowly into a closer (though never perfect) alignment. In prayer, the vector of your purposes comes to be more and more curved toward God.

Two things are certain: most of us pray and most of us think we could pray better. Surveys reveal that a surprisingly high percentage of Americans pray at least occasionally, doubtless often when they find themselves in one of life's foxholes. Prayer is at the heart of Christian practice, but even normally confident and talkative church leaders tremble at the thought of praying out loud at a committee meeting. I have even heard monks who live half of every day on their knees lamenting the poverty of their prayer lives. Jesus' disciples begged him, "Lord, teach us to pray." He responded by teaching them what we call "the Lord's Prayer." The apostle Paul, never one to mince his words, told the Romans, "For we do not know how to pray as we ought." Then he added, "but that very Spirit intercedes with sighs too deep for words."

Prayer begins in just these three places. First, a space for prayer is created by a frank confession that we do not know how to pray so very well. Of all the Beatitudes, the one that comforts me the most is "Blessed are the poor in spirit." The poor in spirit, Jesus knew, were blessed with the one needful thing: They understood that they didn't have it all together spiritually. Second, we find a way into prayer by learning forms and methods of prayer that others have found helpful. Third, prayer comes alive in remembering that it is not finally any technique but "that very Spirit" who quickens and forms prayer in us and then lifts it out of the clay and toward God.

John Calvin said, "Prayer is none other than an expanding of our heart in the presence of God." A child may think of prayer as the task of telling God things, informing the Omniscient One of problems and requests as if God did not already know. We do not tell God anything new in prayer of course; rather, we lay ourselves spiritually bare and make space for a relationship with the Divine Parent. This "communication" moves two ways if we permit it to do so, though usually

only when we stop talking and listen for God. Prayer may involve forms and a certain discipline, but it is not essentially a job that we have to do. We may have to nudge ourselves to make the time in a busy schedule or remember to weave it into the pace of the day, but in the end, prayer is more like play than it is like work.

Nevertheless, when Jesus' disciples asked him to teach them to pray, he did not tell them to be in the presence of God. He taught them a specific short prayer, ostensibly to be memorized. These words themselves have come into every Christian tradition and form a model for other prayers. As the tradition of Christian prayer has evolved, it has suggested five fundamental kinds of prayers:

Prayers of adoration ascribe praise and glory to God. This is the turning away from self and turning toward God the Center that is the core movement of both the life of faith and the act of worship.

Prayers of thanksgiving offer gratitude to God, who is the source of blessing, the giver of all good things, the creator and sustainer of life. Thanksgiving is not so much a single discrete act as it is a basic demeanor toward being.

Prayers of confession do not so much enumerate our individual sins (not possible even for the saints) as they acknowledge our estrangement from ourselves, from others, and from God. We confess not just individual offenses but our need for a right relationship with others, ourselves, and God.

Prayers of supplication articulate our own needs and those of our families and communities. We give voice and shape to our fears and our hopes in the presence of God.

Prayers of intercession are pleas for others, even for the whole world.

One way to discipline our prayer is to include all or most of these types of prayer when we pray. In such a way, we avoid praying out of the self-absorption that would lead to prayers heavy on petition and light on adoration. Prayer may be sung, as it often is in hymns. It may be spoken silently, alone or in common. It may be free, that is, spontaneous and unprepared, or formal. The Lord's Prayer is in this sense a formal prayer. Free prayer may be guided by the Spirit, or it may be guided by the narrowness and self-interest of the person praying. In order to broaden and shape prayer, Christians have turned to several prayer disciplines, some ancient, some more recent.

Praying with Scripture. Traditionally known as *lectio divina* (spiritual reading), this ancient practice weaves readings from the Bible, prayer, and silence together. Alone or in a group, you read a passage slowly, listening for words and phrases that hook your spiritual attention. Then in silence, you meditate on that which spoke to you, asking yourself where it connects with your life. Then you use this observation to shape a prayer, silent or verbalized, ranging from adoration to intercession. Then you rest and simply be in God's presence.

Praying the Psalms. The 150 psalms of the Bible are all prayers, which were first sung and often are today. But as prayers offered alone or in a group, they can simply be read directly or read in a responsive manner. In the Psalms, we pray out the eternal human condition in ancient words that are often sharp and startlingly frank. All the moods of life are laid bare in the Psalms, from fear to trust, from profound joy to bitter anger.

Prayer phrases. I am hopelessly unfocused in my praying. I begin eagerly, but my mind wanders off until all I can do is put a stop to the random wool-gathering with a precipitous "Amen." I have found that short, repeated phrases serve to anchor my drifting mind. When repeated at the opening of a prayer, they serve as a front door, a way to sweep the clutter off the porch. Repeated during prayer, they bring me back into focus. This ancient Christian practice has been rediscovered by many in recent years. The oldest such prayer phrase is probably "Lord, have mercy"; in the Greek, *Kyrie eleison.* A traditional expanded form is often called "the Jesus Prayer": "Lord Jesus Christ, Son of God, have mercy upon me." Some people simply pray "Jesus" or "Come, Holy Spirit." Say one word or phrase as you breathe in; say another as you exhale. In time, prayer becomes like breathing itself, like being itself.

Prayer books. Wonderful resources are available in the form of books of daily prayers for use by individuals or small groups. Prayer books usually offer a structure of Bible readings, prayers, psalms, and sacred actions for the three times of the day most often marked by prayer: morning, evening, and mealtime.

Prayer woven into life. I do a lot of my praying when I drive, not because I'm an especially lousy driver but because it's a chance to pray. I pray when I walk into a meeting that shows every sign of being difficult. I find myself mumbling thankfulness after some gratuitously sweet moment: a cold dip in the lake as the sun goes down, an unmerited conversation with a normally sullen sixteen-year-old. For many, prayer runs over the brim of the formal prayer vessels that would contain it. It is not bound by amens but spills into all life. Prayer is not just the capital letter and the period at either end of the day; prayer comes to be woven into the verbs and nouns of noonday, woven between the prepositions of evening.

But for all the value of such prayer disciplines and structures, in the end, prayer is not a matter of technique. Prayer begins when we admit we can't pray anywhere near well enough. It is often shaped by forms that lead us to try this foreign vocabulary on our unfamiliar tongues. But finally, it is the Presence of God, that Present Tense of God, the Spirit who "intercedes for us with sighs too deep for words" and leads us into the precincts of the Divine. One may have to wait for this Spirit. There is an ancient tradition of "waiting on the Lord," for the well can go dry for years. Your hope for a drop of answered prayer is kept alive only by the rumor of water or your own memory of the taste of water. In time, the Spirit quenches the patiently thirsty. I dare to say this only because so many who have waited have not—in the end—waited in vain.

Chapter 14

Traveling Companions

*T*here was a Christian named Simon who lived in Syria in the early part of the fifth century and longed for closeness to God. He chose a path respected in his day and became a hermit. His search for God led him to isolated clusters of fellow hermits scattered about the deserts of northern Syria. But Simon was convinced that he could only find God by getting away from even his fellow hermits. So in the year 423, when he was about thirty years old, he began to live on a small platform on top of a pillar. At first the pillar was only about twelve feet off the ground, but it was increased in height over the years until it was sixty feet in the air. Simon lived on his isolated perch for the balance of his life, another thirty-six years. This remarkable feat earned him the name Saint Simon Stylites, or Saint Simon of the Pillar.

When I meet with classes of people considering church membership, I have learned to anticipate a question that is often never asked but seems always to be on the minds of many around the circle of folding chairs: "Can I be a Christian on my own, or do I have to join a church?" I answer the question whether or not it gets asked, and I feel compelled to respond honestly. "Yes, you can. It's been done." Sometimes I tell them the story of Simon of the Pillar. Then I add, "But it's extraordinarily difficult, and in spite of all the foibles of church, it's not nearly as much of a joy."

Our modern world's understanding of the individual tends to imagine personhood in isolation, with only incidental reference to others. A person, we think, is the sum of an individual's ideas, passions, strengths, weaknesses, indeed, the "personality" of an individual. Such an individual is viewed in an imaginary solitariness rather than in relationship. Theologian Andrew Purves writes, "In common speech today the word 'person' tends to refer to the self as an individual center of consciousness, a self who is a free subject, a moral agent, one who thinks, feels, acts and so on . . . a privatized, individualized, interiorized sense of self."[1]

Such a definition of self is fundamentally deficient. In reality, our personhood is invariably shaped *in relationship* to other persons. These relationships are not something added on to a fundamentally private self, but relationship is the very thing that has made us into "selves." Our basic nature was formed in relationship and is relationship. Our humanness is drastically misunderstood by defining "person" simply in terms of what goes on inside of us—as if that interior were not shaped by a whole lifetime of "exterior" relationships. As the Scottish philosopher John Macmurray phrased it: "I need 'you' in order to be myself."[2]

Psychologists have long speculated about how children utterly cut off from human relationships might develop. Their speculations were tragically confirmed in recent years when the numerous orphanages of Ceausescu's Romania were opened to the world's eyes after his fall from power. The dictator had mandated bizarre policies that had resulted in thousands of unwanted children. Many of them ended up in vast, underfunded state-run orphanages where they often received no love—often no human contact at all. They were not in relationship with other human beings. The children grew into physical human *creatures* but did not become human *persons*. They could not speak or relate to others; they could not receive or give affection.

The Christian faith understands relationships with others to be of inestimable importance for at least three reasons. First, this is simply how we are made. We are built for relationship. We not only thrive but we become fully human only in relationship with others. Second, Jesus lived his life as a man for others. He lived in community and he loved others so deeply as to lay down his life for them. Third—and here we tread the precincts of mystery—the God we understand in Trinitarian theology is understood not in terms of radical autonomy but in terms of relationship. If the deepest truth about God is that God is relationship, love, and communion, the implications for those who would be in relationship with such a God are stunning. To believe in such a God means that everything "of God" is that which promotes, nourishes, deepens, and sustains relationships of love, trust, communion, and intimacy. Likewise, everything that severs, demeans, trivializes, and hampers such relationships is incongruous with the very nature of God. Such things are not just disobedience of God's *will*, they are in disharmony with the very *being* of God. We who name a Trinitarian God are called to live in relationships of deep communion that are nothing less than an earthly reflection of the life of God.

Church

The church is not a club for those who have arrived, spiritually speaking. Rather, it is a fellowship of spiritual traveling companions who are still very much on the way. We follow Jesus together, and we invariably do so less than perfectly. To join a church does not imply that you have finally reached some requisite level of spiritual high-jumping. It means that you are ready to make the leap of faith. Joining a church does not mean that you know all the answers; it means that you are committed to follow One about whom questions may linger but whose call you can no longer ignore. You do not know everything about him; you only know enough to trust him as Lord and Savior.

Church becomes a community that incarnates both love within that fellowship and love for the larger world. In spite of dull committee meetings and stretched budgets, in spite of difficult pastors and insufferable fellow members, life together can become a foretaste of the sweet promise of the perfect community implicit in the Triune God. Sunday worship, Tuesday Women's Circle, Wednesday staff meeting, the Thursday night homeless meal, the Habitat for Humanity project Saturday morning, the senior high ski trip—all of it so far from perfect—are as tuneful a whisper of true community as we're likely to hear in this world.

Choosing a church to join—"church shopping"—just isn't what it used to be. There was a day when Presbyterians new in town went directly to First Presbyterian—no checking out several local pastors' sermons, no comparative inquiries about youth programs. For better or worse, the old denominational loyalties that long shaped the American church scene are weakening. People visit churches of different denominations. They comparison shop, looking for the right minister, a theology that fits them, worship that inspires, and a lively Sunday school program for the kids. Competition has been good for the auto industry. Whether or not it ultimately turns out to be good for churches is yet to be seen, but to my mind there is something backward about this search for the right church. When I meet with folks in those same new-member classes, I acknowledge church shopping and get a knowing laugh. I confess, "You have a right to ask what this church can offer you. But there is another question you ought to ask. And it's not the second question, but the first. You need to ask what you can offer the church."

Marriage and Family

Intimacy comes in a plethora of amazing shapes. Among them all, the church has long seen fit to bless marriage and family in a particular way. Whether or not we marry, we all participate in family, for all of us are children and grandchildren. Family is the universal of the human community, and as such Christian faith has attended closely to it. This is true in spite of the fact that Jesus probably never married and that the apostle Paul has rather little to say about the institution. Ironically, the most famous biblical families are those of the Old Testament patriarchs—Abraham, Isaac, and Jacob—any of which might be judged dysfunctional by a modern family therapist.

Christian faith's concern for family rises from several sources. First, family relationships obviously form and touch all of us. Second, family matters because of the truth that we explored in the preceding pages. Our full humanity, our fundamental identity and very personhood, is found in relationships. For most of us, no network of relationships is more formative than the families we came from and may now participate in. Finally, Christians have come to understand that the kind of human relationship that builds us into our fullest humanity is the same kind of relationship that God has shown to us, especially in the story of Israel and the life of Jesus. The main mark of those revelatory relationships is a love that is enduringly faithful and self-giving. The marks of most happy marriages and solid families are the same: enduring faithfulness and self-giving love.

I used to ask couples in premarital counseling sessions to describe the give-and-take of their relationship in terms of percentages. They always looked at me as if I were none too bright and glibly answered, "50–50, of course." Then I would press them: "Really? Is it always exactly equal?" They would usually admit that it was not 50–50 all the time but then would insist that it averaged out at 50–50. This gave me my opportunity. "In a lifetime of marriage—after fifty years or more— you may be able to look back and say that it averaged out equally, but I rather doubt it, frankly. Life is seldom so mathematically tidy. But the real point is this: It doesn't matter very much if it's equal or not. Marriage isn't a business deal. The real joy will come not in some unlikely balance. It will come in giving, even sacrificing to each other."

All this becomes true in spades for those who have children. If you did not learn the lesson in marriage, you learn it in the spiritual graduate school of parenthood. Your joy rises and falls with that of little human beings whom you love as you love your own life. The birth and nurture of children is a spiritual watershed for many. Up close and personally, you witness the fearsome dangers and unspeakable wonders of life. With the birth of a child, you are promoted to awesome responsibilities and step one rung higher on the ladder of mortality. The moment your first child comes into the world, you are no longer a member of the youngest generation.

In a world that has gravitated toward disposable relationships, the Christian faith has insisted on the importance of endurance and faithfulness. Divorce is always a tragedy. Usually no one knows that better than those who feel they have no alternative but to end their marriages. Some parts of the church have come to accept divorce as the best course for some hopelessly broken relationships, but always sorrowfully and reluctantly.

Martin Luther, who married happily, once named marriage "a school for the soul." For many, marriage is the best chance they ever get to grow out of self-orientation into an abiding concern for at least one other human being. In marriage, you must grow beyond life as a little clod of earth forever complaining that the world will not devote itself to making you happy. You are pressed by the intimacies of the days to understand one great truth: that your happiness really is bound up in the happiness of another, your personal fulfillment is inseparable from the fulfillment of other human beings.

Friendship

Abiding friendship is modeled more frequently in the Bible than are happy marriages. The most powerful illustration of friendship is shown in the relationship between Jesus and his disciples, whom he calls "friends" rather than servants (John 15:15). Friendship, both for those who marry and those who are called to the single life, is shaped by the same high claims that form the communities of church and family: the insistence that friendship is not just a matter of "having some company." Friendships, like marriages and the community of faith, are a place where we become who we are. And like marriage, friendship is at its fullest when it grows into enduring faithfulness and is graced with the yielding of self for the friend.

I recall watching two kinds of birds during my high school years along Lake Michigan: seagulls and Canada geese. The gulls walked the hard limestone shelves along the shore and always flew alone. They would rise high with the breeze off the lake, then swoop down to skim the surface of the water. They looked magnificently free. They would follow the fishing boats coming into Manistique harbor in the late afternoons, a raucous gray and white mob looking for fishy handouts cast from the sterns of the boats. Whenever they were together, gulls were either squabbling over fish guts or fighting about who got to sit on what dock piling.

Canada geese are different. Twice a year, hundreds of thousands of them would pass overhead on their way to the Seney National Wildlife Refuge north of town. Some fall days, the sky would be black with geese. Seldom would you see one alone. They usually fly in their famous V-formation. In so doing, scientists say that they can actually fly 71 percent farther than they could alone. The bird ahead creates lift that makes it easier for the bird just behind. Canada geese even have a system of rotating leadership so that the burden of being in the lead is shared. And if a bird becomes ill and has to drop out of formation, another member of the flock will always stay behind.

We are fashioned by a Creator (who *is* relationship) in such a way that our humanity is discovered in relationship. As such, we are "created in the image of God."

Chapter 15

As Good as You Get

A member of a high school confirmation class walked into a young minister's office. He was the only person in the class who was not only to be confirmed but also to be baptized in church the next day. Baptism begs some particular pastoral attention, so the minister had asked the boy to visit her office late on Saturday morning so that they could talk about the sacrament of baptism in general and his baptism the next day in particular.

He came in fresh from soccer practice—sweaty and smelly—sat down, and swung his bare legs as the minister carefully outlined the theology and practice of the Christian sacrament of baptism. She talked about how things would work in the service the next morning. At this point, the young man broke into her well-organized presentation and said, "I'm going out to the lake with a couple of friends this afternoon. Why not get baptized there today?" The minister reached to her bookshelf and pulled out a volume on the sacraments and church policy to explain all the good reasons why baptism is generally in church on a Sunday and not at the lake on Saturday afternoon. As she was looking for the reference, she thought to ask this insightful question: "If you got baptized out there away from folks in the church, how would they ever know that you'd been baptized?" Without skipping a beat, the boy answered, "Why, by the way I act, of course."

He may not have understood the church rules, but the kid understood that ethical behavior lies at the heart of the Christian life. The faith has always insisted that two things are true about the moral life. At first they seem to be in some tension with each other, but the truth is that any system of ethics which neglects either becomes thin moral ice. The first observes that the problem with human behavior is more serious than you might think. The second affirms that people really can change anyway.

Even though the faith is full of hope for changing people, it does not follow that Christians are basically "optimistic" about human nature. Christian tradition is relentlessly realistic about the human potential for everything from the unspeakable evil of the Holocaust to the peevishness of the lonely old lady in the green bungalow across the street. The traditional word to describe this reality has come to be singularly unfashionable. For most of us, that *outré* little word "sin" invokes images of angry preachers thundering their accusatory sermons, gaunt and angry Elmer Gantrys balancing an open Bible in one hand and pointing a bony finger with the other.

How sin came to be such an unpopular notion is an important story. Before it slipped into the pejorative tones that ring in the ears of most who now hear the word, *sin* was the simple word used to describe the reality that things are not as they ought to be, that we too often live estranged from each other and from God. I offer thumbnail sketches of three of the thinkers whose ideas about what's wrong with the world have helped to nudge the idea of sin off the stage of respectable ideas. First, the Swiss-born French philosopher of the early Enlightenment, Jean-Jacques Rousseau, responded to the "what's wrong" question by saying that culture and society have messed us up. Humanity in its primitive and natural stage was and is pure as snow. Rousseau invented the phrase "the noble savage." All we need to do is to scrap tradition, throw culture out the window, dump society as we know it, start over, and everything will be fine. The French Revolution proved him disastrously wrong.

Second, Karl Marx said that the problem is the gap between the rich and the poor. After the revolution, when everything is fair, a new humanity will emerge. The state and its laws will wither away and we'll all live happily ever after. Events of the last century showed the world how wrong he was.

Finally, Sigmund Freud, the father of psychoanalysis, responded to the question by intimating that the problem lies in childhood experiences. Work through the traumas of unresolved guilt, preadolescent sexuality, and overly aggressive toilet training, and a healthy new personality will emerge. Right or wrong, the pressing question is how we get all of the world's six billion people into psychoanalysis at the same time!

These thinkers, at least Marx and Freud, are great lights in the history of ideas. Marx, in spite of the unraveling of communism, contributed to the way we understand history. Freud engendered a whole tradition of reflection about the interior self that has amplified even the Christian faith and helped countless people to find emotional health. But when it comes to an answer to the "what's wrong" question, they all fall short.

This point was eloquently made in a 1987 film about China, *The Last Emperor,* based on the life of the last emperor before the Marxist revolution, Pu Ye. Toward the end of the film, there is a scene set in the early 1950s in a Communist re-education prison camp. Pu Ye asks the commandant of the camp, a good man and a Marxist true-believer, why they are bothering to put him through this nine-year program of forced indoctrination into Marxist-Leninist theory. The commandant replies, his voice raised and his face close to his former emperor: "Because we believe that all people are basically good; they have just been taught bad habits." That's not only a classic Marxist answer, it's an answer that would have pleased Rousseau, perhaps even Freud. I fear that it's probably still the most popular answer of our age.

But just a few moments later, the entire prison camp is shown watching re-education films that graphically portray Japanese atrocities during the war. We see mass executions in Shanghai and brutal biological warfare experiments in Manchuria. Pu Ye, the last emperor, who in spite of his collaboration with the Japanese knew nothing of this, rises from his seat and stares incredulously at the horrors on the screen. The commandant's words ring shallow and naive: "We believe that all people are basically good; they have just been taught bad habits."

At the very end of the film, years after Pu Ye has been released from the prison camp, we meet that optimistic prison commandant again. The year is 1967 and now he has been arrested by the zealous and arrogant young Red Guards because of some flaw in his ideological orthodoxy. He is being marched through the streets of Beijing, handcuffed, wearing a dunce's cap. The former keeper of prisoners is now the prisoner of another generation of true believers who will try him and punish him for not believing quite the right thing. His own words ring hollow and naive: "We believe that all people are basically good; they have just been taught bad habits."

Much of the ethical thinking of modernism—from Rousseau to Freud and beyond—has effectively externalized sin. "What's wrong" is not in me; it's out there. I do bad things, other people do bad things, because of our culture, our history, our upbringing, maybe even our genes. The problem is parents who pushed too hard or not hard enough, schools too strict or not strict enough, being reared in poverty or growing up surrounded by unchecked materialism, or maybe it was just an older brother who got all the attention.

The word *sin* rings harshly in our ears because it means that "what's wrong" has to do with me. "What's wrong" is at least partly my fault, or, more accurately, it is related to my "faultiness." I recall an old chestnut about an elderly pillar of the church who had just had the doctrine of sin uncompromisingly explained to her: how sin means the problem was not "out there" but "in us," and how complex and comprehensive sin is, how it has a way of creeping into everything we do, even finding its way into our noblest acts. After this explanation she is said to have exclaimed, "Well, if we're as bad off as all that, God help us."

Which is precisely the point. God help us. The Christian faith may be insistently realistic about human nature, but it is boundlessly hopeful about the possibility that people can change. Change is possible not because the problem is slight; it is possible because with God, all things are possible. The ethical life looks inward to face the depth of the challenge and then looks outward to God for strength. In the sixth chapter of his letter to the Romans, Paul says that such change can become real through the central drama of the Christian faith: death and resurrection. In order for people to really change, something must die: Old habits of the heart must die, fear and self-centeredness must die, complaining and peevishness must die, anger and hatefulness must die. All this Paul names the "sinful body." He puts it starkly. All that which is sin—meaning estrangement from God, others, and self—must be crucified, dead, and buried. Still grounded in that central crucifixion and resurrection drama, Paul says that people can be raised to new life by the power of God. I'm not especially confident that people really change much by their own effort, but they can "walk in newness of life," as Paul phrases it, because they can be changed by the grace and power of God, which are eternally dramatized in the resurrection. This is no mere "bringing out the best" in people, no human-potential-movement optimism about basic human goodness. This is the stark affirmation that if people are going to change, something has got to go—"crucified, dead, and buried." Only then can the new be raised up.

Can those twisted hearts who burn African American churches be changed? Can seriously screwed-up kids grow into happy adults? Can self-absorbed adults become people of spiritual substance? Yes—I've seen it happen. Paul saw it happen in his own life. But that potential for change was hardly lodged in the heart of the old Paul who watched Stephen being stoned to death. The potential for change is not necessarily sleeping in the souls of the hate-filled shouters whose faces fill the evening news. But there is power for change, the spark, the love, the grace burns hot in the heart of God. They may not have it in them to change, but God has it in God to change them.

Obedience

God raises us into a new moral life in at least three ways. The first way is obedience. God has given the gift of the law, rules revealed in Scripture to shape behavior. The two central laws of Scripture are the Ten Commandments and Jesus' Great Commandment: "You shall love the Lord your God with all your heart, and with all your soul, and with all your mind. . . . You shall love your neighbor as yourself."

In any discussion of the moral law, several things must be kept in mind. Religious laws are not the essence of Christian ethics, much less the Christian life. The Swiss physician and religious essayist Paul Tournier tells of a pastor who asked the students in his confirmation class a simple starter question: "What is religion?" One young boy's hand popped into the air. With not a doubt in his little head, he answered, "Religion shows us the things we must not do." He may have been quick, but he was a mile wide of the target. More than a few people have been spiritually scarred after being beaten about the soul with some form of religious legalism. But even if moral laws are not the essence of faith, they make it clear to those who take them seriously and then look honestly at their own lives that there is a major shortfall between what God commands and what they actually do. In this way, the law serves to challenge us to face the fact that our lives miss the mark.

Finally, even though we know that perfect obedience is not humanly possible, law serves us as a welcome guide. In Scripture, the law is always understood as a gift, not a burden. Law does not limit human possibilities but charts a deepwater channel that leads us safely into more abundant life. It is designed not to constrict our possibilities but to keep us off the rocks. To use another nautical metaphor, the law, if it be a burden, is the kind of burden that sails are for a ship.

We are a lot like a child who has just opened his main gift on Christmas morning. This year's main gift is some complicated mechanical or electronic toy in a box that notes circumspectly, "Some assembly required." The child bursts with excitement and rips the toy out of its molded Styrofoam packing. Mom says, "Slow down, kiddo, let's sit down and read the directions together. I'll show you how it works." The child answers, "I want to do it all by myself," and trots off behind the couch, leaving the directions lying in Dad's lap. In twenty minutes, the child is back, angry and frustrated, on the edge of tears. The stupid thing doesn't work. Nothing fits together right. One of the pieces is already busted.

Life is one complicated main gift. Some assembly is indeed required. Our first thought is to put it together alone, to make it work all by ourselves. We may seem to get it together for a moment, but then something goes awry. We struggle to figure the thing out—what plugs into what, where all the odd little pieces go—but it only gets more frustrating. The stupid thing just doesn't work. Nothing fits together right. One piece is already broken. Then, just maybe, we remember that it came with directions. They're around here somewhere. And more than that, we may remember that there is one very patient parent sitting on the other side of the couch waiting, just waiting, to help us put it together.

Imitation

A second way in which God teaches us how to walk ethically is at least as old as Thomas à Kempis's fifteenth-century spiritual classic, *The Imitation of Christ*, and as young as the bracelet that my daughter wore around her wrist that read, "WWJD," shorthand for "What would Jesus do?" Law challenges us to face the challenge and then guides us. But beyond the law, God offers us real human lives to imitate. A piece of the mosaic of ethical formation, especially for the young, has always been heroes—men and women worthy of emulation. For a long period in the history of the church, and still today in some traditions, books called "Lives of Saints" were the core curriculum of devotional reading. Of course, for all Christians, Jesus Christ is the central figure of ethical imitation. Our time has grown cynical about heroes. So many professional athletes seem to have ethical Achilles' heels. The glaring light of the media has revealed the moral frailties of political and religious figures, both past and present.

As important to the faith as the ethic of imitation has been and is, it has two intrinsic shortcomings. First, sometimes it is difficult to imagine what Jesus, for example, might do in the kinds of situations we face. In a world of computers and nuclear fission, it is often nearly impossible to stretch your moral imagination far enough to say confidently what Jesus, who lived his life as a Galilean peasant, would do if his feet were in your Nikes. Second, and more important, it is obviously not the case that I am always supposed to do exactly what Jesus did. Jesus did not marry. Does this imply that I shouldn't? Jesus lived a life of poverty. Does this imply that all his followers should be poor? Jesus died willingly on the cross. Does this imply that his disciples are always called to martyrdom? Though it has its place, the ethic of imitation can be as frustrating as that of obedience. A figure worthy of imitation will always be one whom we can imitate no more perfectly than we can obey the law.

Inspiration

Spirit is hidden in the middle of the word *inspiration.* And Spirit is hidden in the heart of the ethical life. Christian faith claims that not only does God offer laws and lives to guide and imitate but that God's Spirit works in us to make moral discernment fit for our time. This same Spirit then strengthens us to discern and do what is right. In this third movement, ethics become not simply a matter of conforming your life to historical commandments or imitating others' lives. The ethical life also becomes an experience of formation in the numinous hands of a Presence now active in your life. In the fourteenth chapter of John's Gospel, as Jesus sits with his friends on the last night of his life, he anticipates their need for such a Spirit. "I have said these things to you while I am still with you. But the Advocate, the Holy Spirit, whom the Father will send in my name, will teach you everything, and remind you of all that I have said to you" (John 14:25–26).

God does not intend to press us into uniformity. This is to say, if all of the followers of Jesus were somehow suddenly enabled to live lives of perfect obedience, if they were all to properly imitate their Lord, if they attended precisely the Spirit working in their lives, they would not all be alike. God obviously revels in wild variety, not only among orchids and beetles but in humans as well. Our gifts are as diverse as the shape of our noses, and to attend to the Spirit will lead those who listen not toward conformity but into transformation into the unique human being they were created to be. The great Jewish theologian Martin Buber once remarked about himself, "In the Day of Judgment, the Lord will not ask me, 'Why were you not more like Moses or Elijah?' Rather, the Lord will ask me, 'Why were you not more like Martin Buber?'"

A Good Word for Hypocrisy

A charge often leveled at people who are serious about religious faith is that they are "a bunch of hypocrites." At one level, the accusation is perfectly true. Christians struggle to live their lives in the light of a radical ethic, and not even the most saintly ever comes close to doing it perfectly. The more serious you are about it, the better you know how far from the mark you are. If having an ethic that is so demanding that it cannot be perfectly lived is hypocrisy, then we *are* a bunch of hypocrites. In fact, there are only three kinds of people who are not hypocrites: those who are perfect, those who have no moral standards at all, and those whose standards are low enough for them to always reach. The truly sinister form of hypocrisy is always pretense. Pretense is giving the impression that you actually are living up to the ethical demands you espouse.

I have a second contrary observation about hypocrisy. If it is hypocrisy to hold your peace when you feel like verbally slicing a tired receptionist to bloody ribbons, we are called to be hypocrites. If it is hypocrisy to put your hands in your pockets when everything in you wants to box your rude fourteen-year-old in the ear, we are called to be hypocrites. Time and again, the ethical life demands that we "try on" behavior that is at odds with what we feel like doing.

But are these really the only alternatives: always doing the right thing even if you don't feel it inside, or always doing just what you feel like? Imbedded in the gospel is a third way, the gutsy affirmation that dark little hearts can be changed. You can actually come to *want* to do the right thing. The gospel trusts that hearts can be reshaped by the Spirit of a God who loves us as we are but wants us to grow into more. The down-to-earth reality, of course, is that my heart is often bringing up the rear, morally speaking. I don't always feel like saying that impossibly kind word. So the practical question is this: Do I wait for the Spirit to change my heart before I start acting like it's being changed? Or do I do what I know to be right even though a big part of me feels like doing something else? This is an everyday dilemma, and into it the faith speaks a commandment and a promise: Speak the kind word, do the right thing, even if it isn't the first word or the only act in your heart. That's the commandment. Then comes the promise: Wait for your heart to catch up with your actions.

The author Max Beerbohm retold a morally pointed version of the children's classic "Beauty and the Beast" in a short story called "The Happy Hypocrite." His tale is about "a regency rake" named Lord George Hell, a debauched and shameless sinner, who falls wildly in love with a saintly young girl. To win her love, Lord George covers his bloated features with the mask of a saint. The girl is deceived and becomes his bride. They live together happily until a woman from Hell's wicked past turns up and exposes him. She challenges him to take off his mask. Sadly, and having no choice, he takes it off only to find that beneath the saint's mask is the face of the saint he has become by wearing it in love.

A Good Word for Love

The New Testament scholar Krister Stendahl wrote a wise and witty little essay called "The Ten Commandments for Biblical Preaching." His ninth commandment was to the effect that: "You shall not use the word 'love' unless it is in the text," that is, in the Bible reading for the day. Stendahl quipped that his ninth commandment "sobers up preaching wonderfully." I tremble at drawing this chapter to a close with "love" because the word has been handled so much it is worn thin. Too many preachers and romance novelists have fondled it into sentimentality.

Sentimentality concentrates its attention too much on warm and kind feelings without paying sufficient attention to the hard and grim realities of the human experience. It is stunningly ironic that Christian love could ever be smoothed into sentimentality because planted squarely in the heart of this faith are two realities: First, Jesus commanded us to love; you cannot exactly command warm feelings. Second, at the heart of this faith is the cross, that high-water mark in the flood of all the hard realities that sentimentalism would ignore.

When I meet with engaged couples to talk about marriage, we always spend one session going over the wedding service itself. We read it through together and talk about the words that will be spoken to and by them. One question always arises in this discussion. If they don't bring it up, I do. It seems odd to couples—usually young and in love—that the wedding service barely mentions love at all. They sometimes ask, "Isn't our wedding a celebration of our love?"

"Not precisely," I answer. The wedding service assumes your love. It is a given. Love is the raw material you bring. You bring that powerful emotion, your passion for each other, to marriage. But in the wedding service, the word of the day is not love. The words that predominate in the liturgy are "vow" and "commitment" and "promise" and "covenant." Marriage begins with the "feeling" of love. But like any feeling, it has its up days and its down days. Feelings can be notoriously erratic, rising and falling with mood and fortune. Marriage takes this powerful if variable emotion and hardens it, tempers it, grows it, into something deeper and more lasting. "Commitment," "promise," "covenant," "vow" are the words that the wedding service uses to talk about growing love into something that outlasts the vagaries of emotion. Commitment throws a bridge over love's dark valleys. Promise is what keeps you present when you feel emotionally numb. Covenant keeps you there until the passion reawakens and grows stronger than before. Commitment pulls love beyond sentiment. This is not just true for love within marriage, for what is true in marriage is true in all relationships of commitment.

The core of Christian ethics is a tough and insistent love. This love draws into itself the three gifts that God has given us to guide us in the Way: obedience, imitation, and inspiration. When asked to name the greatest commandment in the law, Jesus answered that it was love for God and neighbor. That answer was not meant to be simply descriptive; it is a proscriptive commandment for those who would follow. Love is not simply a feeling; it is an act of will, a commitment to act. If it were mere feeling, it could be neither commanded nor obeyed.

Love also imitates. Jesus' followers are called to emulate Christ, not in the details of his life but in the way he loved. His was a love that both turned the other cheek and rebuked Pharisees. His was a love that drew little children into its arms and stretched its arms out on a cross. You and I are hardly called to imitate the cultural details of his life. Difficult as that would be, it would be easy compared to stepping in the long, strong strides of his love.

In the end, we can neither obey nor imitate well enough to love perfectly. We need something beyond ourselves, an inspiration beyond mortal efforts at obedience and imitation. We need a Love larger than our love. This need can become reality in that Present Tense of God, the Holy Spirit, who we may find, to our surprise, is so tireless and so subtle that the Spirit might love even us—however jaded and skeptical we may be—into a love that we thought was not in us.

Chapter 16

Seventy Times Seven

*D*avid Noel Freedman is the kind of Bible scholar who can recite obscure chapters of the Old Testament from memory—in Hebrew. Now an elderly man, he lives with one foot planted in Judaism and the other in Christianity. His life has been immersed in the study of Scripture. Once asked if all he had learned could be summed up in one sentence, he thought for but a moment and answered, "There is forgiveness."

The forgiveness that runs like marbled veins through the bedrock of Scripture moves in two directions. It cuts vertically and it splinters out horizontally. Our faith trusts that it runs downward from God to this world and then spiders outward, horizontally, as one forgiven soul forgives another. For people of faith, those two movements are necessarily interrelated. My own ability to forgive is quickened by God's forgiveness of me.

Jesus fuses the two together in Matthew 18. Peter had asked him a question: "If another member of the church sins against me, how often should I forgive? As many as seven times?" It was an honest and practical kind of query. It suggested that seven times would be plenty indulgent. Some religious traditions had indeed set an upper limit on forgiveness. But Jesus answers, "Not seven times, but, I tell you, seventy-seven times." That figure is an indirect way of saying that there is no outer limit on forgiveness. Then Jesus tells a story that forever connects the vertical and the horizontal vectors of forgiveness. It is a simple parable with a hard edge. A man is forgiven an immense debt by his master, the king. No sooner has the guy bounded to the bottom of the palace steps with sighs of relief than he is approached by a debtor who owes him pocket change and who asks for forgiveness. Our man on the steps stops, thinks, and refuses. He is somehow blind to the connection between receiving and giving forgiveness.

Forgiven

I honestly don't know which is harder: to forgive the unforgivable, or to accept forgiveness when you think you're unforgivable. Clearly, Jesus perceived that receiving forgiveness ought to exercise the spiritual muscle it takes to forgive others. Yet people sometimes rebuff the forgiveness of God. They deny their forgivability, or, more accurately, they underestimate the grace of God and choose to live bearing the weight of unresolved guilt. One can but speculate that their burden comes to function as a perverse kind of penance; the weight of guilt becomes a self-imposed sentence.

In Will Campbell's memoir of the civil rights movement, *Brother to a Dragonfly*, the author narrates the ongoing banter between himself, "Preacher Will," and his old friend, "P.D.," a small-town newspaper editor and hard-drinking agnostic, a man who struggles to be good and often is but can never quite come to accept himself. P.D. is forever giving Preacher Will a hard time about religion. In one scene, P.D. dares Preacher Will to define Christianity in ten words. Will resists such draconian editing of the gospel, but P.D. badgers him into giving it a try. Finally, he chooses his words: "We're all bastards, but God loves us anyway." P.D. likes the definition, though he notes that Will has two words left over.

In a more literary vocabulary, in his novel *The Heart of the Matter*, Graham Greene quotes Rainer Maria Rilke: "We are all falling. This hand is falling, too—all have this falling sickness none withstands. And yet there's always One whose gentle hands this universal falling can't fall through." Professor Freedman condensed the great story of Scripture into a declaration that from Genesis to Revelation, the first and last word is forgiveness. This is no mere footnote to the Divine. Grace, he is saying, is God's middle name. And so it is true that to refuse forgiveness is actually to refuse God whose very nature is to forgive.

An old Hasidic tale tells the story of a rabbi and his disciples whose common purse was down to the last coin. Passing into their village, they stumbled upon a beggar, not the pitiable kind but a man of ill repute. The rabbi pulled out their only coin and gave it to the man. His disciples were incredulous. "Why would you give everything we had to an undeserving rascal like this?" they asked. The rabbi answered, "Do I dare be any choosier than was God who gave it to me?"

Forgiving

Forgiveness is needful not only for the healing of souls but for the healing of the world. Bishop Desmond Tutu of South Africa fought the brutality of apartheid for most of his life. He took the blows of racism for decades, was tried on trumped-up charges in kangaroo courts, and spent years in jail. He then served as a member of his country's Truth and Reconciliation Commission. The Commission labored through the horrific details of South Africa's painful history of atrocities, false arrests, and summary executions. Tutu summed up what has to happen in six hard words: "There is no future without forgiveness."

There is no future for the world without forgiveness. No future for South Africa without forgiveness. No future for America without forgiveness. No future for the Middle East without forgiveness. No future for Northern Ireland without forgiveness. No future for Iraq without forgiveness.

And what is true on a geopolitical scale is just as true for you and me on the personal scale. There is no future for us without forgiveness. How many lives I have watched eaten away by the acid of unforgiven hurt! Every one of us has watched people—maybe ourselves—hold on to some old offense like a hot coal in the palm of the hand. We understand that there is no future for the world without forgiveness. We know that the old ethic of tit for tat only condemns the world to more of the same. We know that individual lives are spiritually mummified by years of holding on to unforgiven hurts. We know this, but we hesitate to accept the invitation to the dance of grace.

Often we don't want to dance for what appear to be good reasons. It's sometimes extraordinarily difficult to forgive. We declare with some candor that we simply "don't have it in our hearts." And even if our hearts are ready, our heads ask if sometimes we forgive so soon and easily that we diminish the enormity of the offense. How soon—if ever—can the sole survivor in a Cambodian family forgive Pol Pot and the Khmer Rouge? Is it true, as a few critics suggested, that forgiveness tripped too easily from the lips of some Christians after the horrific school shootings of the late 1990s? These quandaries yield up some answers only when the meaning of forgiveness is clarified.

First, it is essential to remember that to forgive is not to trivialize. Years ago, I sat in my study with a sensitive woman in her late thirties who had been the victim of a brutal rape as a young adult. Along with other victims, she testified against her rapist, who was convicted and imprisoned. But she told me that the heaviest burden she bore from that day decades earlier was not the memory of the rape; it was her inability to forgive her rapist. As we talked, it gradually became obvious to both of us that her idea of forgiveness had been skewed. In her understanding, forgiveness meant she had to say that what had happened that day was not as horrendous as it was. Forgiveness, she thought, meant that she had to trivialize the offense. For this remarkable woman, the impossible act of forgiveness became possible only when she saw that forgiving and excusing were not the same thing. Too often when we accept an apology, we wave a casual hand and say, "Don't worry, it was nothing," when in fact, it *was* something. To forgive may mean you have to say to yourself, "It did hurt, and by rights, I could just hold on to it. I don't owe you forgiveness, but I choose not to hold on to the anger. I choose to forgive because I want to put the pain behind me and behind you."

Second, we come to a clearer understanding of forgiveness when we remember that it is not just a gift you give to the one you forgive—you also offer the gift to yourself. You give yourself the gift of resolution, even peace, when you choose to set down that hot coal of anger. Frederick Buechner put it like this: "When you forgive somebody who has wronged you, you're spared the dismal corrosion of bitterness and wounded pride."

Third, forgiveness sometimes becomes possible when the people doing the forgiving remember that they stand in need of forgiveness too. The great American theologian Reinhold Niebuhr said, "Forgiving love is a possibility only for those who know they are not good, who feel themselves in need of divine mercy." The world is not divided between the offenders and the offended. The German philosopher Goethe uttered these words in his old age: "One has only to grow older to become more tolerant. I see no fault in others that I might not have committed myself." Sometimes you can forgive the impossible when you remember that you have been impossibly forgiven more times than you can count. Jesus imbedded this very connection in the prayer he taught his followers: "Forgive us our debts, as we forgive our debtors."

Fourth, to forgive is not necessarily to forget. In fit time, it brings health to the soul to forgive the St. Bartholomew's Day Massacre, the Armenian Genocide, and the Holocaust. But they must never be forgotten. They are for us grim and needful lesson books. To set aside national recrimination and our personal burden of old anger does not mean that we must forget history.

Fifth, the Spirit of God is the Spirit of grace, and that Spirit works in us and on us to accomplish that which we could not will on our own. I have heard people say, and I have said myself, "I don't have it in me to forgive." Doubtless this is true, but "in me" is not the only place to look. God has opened many a clenched fist. The only prayer more seemly than asking God for forgiveness is that which asks God for the strength to forgive others.

Without forgiveness there is no hope—no hope for me, no hope for the world. But "there is forgiveness" and there is hope. Jim Lowry, a friend who watches the world with a sharp eye, saw this on an airplane. After boarding the plane and struggling with fellow passengers to find his assigned seat and contort himself into it, he saw an act of true forgiveness.

I wonder now if the woman's name is Grace. She wasn't like the others on the plane. Surely her name is Grace. She sat in seat 18E. At least she finally sat in seat 18E. I was in 19E. I was flying from Memphis to Asheville, a conference on peace and reconciliation. That's when I met the woman . . . didn't really meet her, just saw her, saw her in action. Not quite old enough to be a grandmother, but nice enough to qualify. I'm sure her name is Grace. Grace got on the plane just in line before me and heaved her carry-on luggage in the overhead compartment and settled back in seat 16E. I went back to 19E. Just as I sat down, from the corner of my eye, I caught a flash go by in the aisle. It was a little girl. Then I heard, "Jessica, come back here RIGHT NOW. I'VE HAD IT WITH YOU!"

Then I heard more from Jessica's mom, "LADY, YOU'RE IN MY SEAT."

"Oh, is this not 16E?" said Grace. "I'm so sorry."

"IT'S 16E ALL RIGHT, BUT 16E IS MY SEAT," screamed Jessica's mom. "LET ME SEE YOUR TICKET, LADY," said Jessica's mom as she examined Grace's ticket. "THIS SAYS 18E. ARE YOU BLIND?"

"Oh, I'm so sorry," said Grace. "It must be my bifocals."

"THIS IS ALL I NEED. . . . I'VE HAD IT. . . . COME BACK HERE, JESSICA."

There was a stunned silence over our part of the cabin as Grace resettled herself and her carry-on in 18E and Jessica's mom settled in 16E and strapped Jessica in the seat beside her, saying, "I don't want a peep out of you, young lady."

When we were airborne and the captain had turned off the seat belt sign, Jessica's head popped up over the back of her seat. She was looking back toward Grace. I'm sure her name was Grace. Her name just had to be Grace. Jessica was clutching a Teddy to her cheek with one hand and sucking her thumb on her other hand. Pretty soon Grace waved at Jessica with just one of her fingers. Jessica took her thumb out of her mouth and waved back. Grace made a sign of drying her own tears; Jessica dried her tears. Grace made the signs of patty-cake, patty-cake . . . no words, just the signs. Jessica put down her Teddy and made the signs back. Then Grace made the signs of Teensy Weensy Spider. Jessica made the signs back. Jessica's mom observed all this from the corner of her eye. So it went to Asheville; at least until the captain put the fasten seat belts sign back on.

On the ground in Asheville, a funny thing happened. It was like something had happened to clean the air all around seat 18E. . . . The people all around seat 18E were nice to each other. We helped each other retrieve carry-on luggage. We stood back to let each other in the aisle. We talked to each other in friendly tones. In the terminal I saw Grace and Jessica's mom talking to each other. They were smiling. "See why," Jim said, "I think her name is Grace? It just had to be Grace."

Chapter 17

Deserts and Wild Beasts

Among the patently true things about the journey of life is that it will lead through deserts—fearsome places where wild beasts live. For all its sweetness, life also brings sorrow and disappointment, confusion and illness. Alone among God's creatures, we live knowing that we shall die. Set against the faith's dogged declaration of the goodness of God, these bitter passages ask ageless questions: "If God is good, why do bad things happen?" And more pragmatically: "When they come, how can I find my way through them?" There are no tidy answers to the first question, not in the sense that "three" is the answer to "What's the square root of nine?" But there are responses to both, some more credible than others.

It's God's Will

Some years ago, a young man named Alex Coffin died in a car accident in Boston. His father was William Sloane Coffin, pastor of the Riverside Church in New York City. Thirteen days after he lost his son, he climbed into the pulpit and preached a sermon that began,

> As almost all of you know, a week ago last Monday night, driving in a terrible storm, my son Alexander . . . who enjoyed beating his old man at every game and in every race, beat his father to the grave. . . .
> When a person dies, there are many things that can be said, and there is at least one thing that should never be said. The night after Alex died I was sitting in the living room of my sister's house outside

Boston, when the front door opened and in came a nice-looking lady with about eighteen quiches. When she saw me she shook her head, then headed for the kitchen, saying sadly over her shoulder, "I just don't understand the will of God. . . ." The one thing that should never be said when someone dies is "It is the will of God." Never do we know enough to say that. My own consolation lies in knowing that it was not the will of God that Alex die; that when the waves closed over his sinking car, God's heart was the first of all our hearts to break.[1]

The will of God is a mystery beyond not only these brief pages but finally beyond all the ink ever shed over the topic. The central witness of Scripture and the consistent witness of men and women who have felt God stirring in their lives is that God's overarching will toward us is born in love and shaped by mercy. "If God is for us," Paul rhetorically inquired of the Romans, "who is against us?" To blithely assign God the role as the indifferent executor of all things is to imagine a God of moral ambivalence. Such a being is foreign to the Bible and to the experience of the faithful. To assign every last thing to the will of God tidies up the ambiguities of the universe but posits a God who is hard to love.

But equally foreign to Christian tradition is a God who is powerless over the unfolding events in the world. We name God "omnipotent," which means "all-powerful," a radical confession to the effect that God could do whatever God might choose. Such a confession does not imagine God sitting coolly in heaven and wiggling a divine finger so that two cars might collide on the corner of Church and Main. It is a confession that somehow all things are wrapped up in an impenetrable providence, a movement of God's will that tacks back and forth into the eye of the storm toward a blessed destination not on our maps but hidden in the divine mind. "We know that all things work for good," Paul assured the Romans. So it is that we live set between the rock of a good and all-powerful God and the hard place of a world in which bad things do indeed happen to good people.

It's Not Partly Cloudy; It's Partly Sunny

Another venerable response to the deserts and the beasts is to commend an attitude of dogged optimism: "Grit your teeth; it's really not so bad after all." "Look on the bright side." "The glass is half full, not half empty." "It's partly sunny, not partly cloudy." You can only admire chipper people, but in the end I cannot face a middle-aged woman who is approaching surgery for ovarian cancer, a dozen radiation treatments, and a grim prognosis and tell her to "look on the bright side." I cannot tell a young couple with a child just diagnosed with cystic fibrosis that "the glass is half full." Whether chosen or natural, an optimistic attitude is indeed a winsome virtue, but as a final answer it dries up in life's Saharas.

I Found God in My Desert

Yes, very often you do find God there. There is a long tradition of going to the "desert," both literally and metaphorically, to find God. God, of course, lives there no more than in the oases, but in the leanness of parched landscape, Divinity is often more easily spotted. I blame neither the deserts nor the beasts on God, but I trust that God does not hesitate to speak in and through them. The terrible stillness of the desert allows us to hear the Voice lost in noisier landscapes. We are held still by experiences of vulnerability that alert us to the possibility of the Transcendent: the death of a parent, a painful divorce, recovery from addiction, a sudden illness, the loss of a job, a numbing bout with despair. In such passages where the road grows rough and the miles desperately fearsome, providence may bring us face to face with that space in us long aching for Spirit.

Søren Kierkegaard was a Danish philosopher, unlucky in love and eccentric by any standard. Often named the father of existentialist philosophy, he was also a Christian who lived his faith in vehement reaction to the bourgeois church of nineteenth-century Denmark. Kierkegaard wrote from experience that every Christian has points in his journey where he feels utterly empty, desert times when his soul is hungry and thirsty for Spirit.

Thomas Merton, who became a poet, theologian, mystic, and Trappist monk, had just graduated from high school when he went alone on a tour of Europe. His father had just died and he had been leading a dissolute life. He would later tell the story of that night in a hotel room, alone and on the run spiritually, when he entered into an emotional and spiritual crisis that became for him his desert.

I was filled with horror at what I saw and my whole being rose up in revolt against what was within me, and my soul desired escape and liberation and freedom from all this with an intensity and urgency unlike anything I had ever known before. And now I think for the first time in my whole life I really began to pray—praying to the God I had never known, to reach down towards me out of His darkness and help me.[2]

Poet and essayist Kathleen Norris was raised in the church and then left the faith for many years, only to find her way back to Christ in her thirties. In *Amazing Grace*, she writes of an acquaintance, a brilliant young scholar who was stricken with cancer and over the course of several years came close to dying three times. But after extensive treatments, both radiation and chemotherapy, came a welcome remission. Her prognosis was uncertain at best, but she was able to teach again. "I'd never want to go back," she told her department head, an older woman, "because now I know what each morning means, and I am so grateful to be alive." When the other woman said to her, "We've been through so much together in the last few years," the younger woman nodded, and smiled. "Yes," she said emphatically, "yes! And hasn't it been a blessing!"[3]

Life's desert passages often open us up to what had been hidden to our eyes in green valleys. Jesus said as much when he flatly declared, "Those who are well have no need of a physician, but those who are sick; I have come to call not the righteous but sinners" (Mark 2:17). I am not so sure that God occasions those passages through sickness in body or soul, but I know that God does not hesitate to speak through them.

The Bayeux Tapestry records in woven pictures and words one of the great events of European history—the Battle of Hastings at which the Norman duke, William the Conqueror, defeated the English king and his armies. In one scene, William's brother, Bishop Odon, is portrayed prodding the soldiers into the fray with his lance tip aimed at their posteriors. The Latin caption above the scene reads, "Odon comforts the men." It is the old meaning of the word "comfort," of course: *con fortis*, "with strength." So also God may comfort us in the fray.

Though God may use the desert and speak through the beasts for our best, their usefulness hardly justifies their existence. In his early writings, C. S. Lewis made what he thought was a good case for the deserts and the beasts. He named such experiences "God's alarm clock." Suffering, he said, was God's way of arresting the attention of somnolent souls and alerting us irresistibly to the deeper things. It was his wife's cancer and subsequent death that disheveled this tidy explanation of suffering. *Shadowlands* is a play about Lewis's marriage to Joy Davidman and her difficult death a few years later. In a powerful soliloquy, Lewis faces the audience with Joy lying in a hospital bed in the background. He confesses that his "alarm clock" theology had been too glib. No theory explains what she has suffered. He confesses that there are too many pains far too sharp ever to be justified by what they might teach us.

The deserts and the beasts are real. You know the names of yours. I cannot look you in the eye and tell you that they're for your own good. But I can tell you that by the grace of God you may be able to wrench something from the teeth of the beast: some quickening for the soul, some lost truth, some elusive maturity. This is not to say that God sends every beast into our desert, even if the encounter may be for some good. Some grow embittered, jaded, and broken in the desert; some grow the other way, newly compassionate, grounded in love, freshly inclined toward God and neighbor. Most of us have little choice of the beast. Perhaps the only choice is how the meeting changes us. In the desert passages, two questions present themselves: "Why?" and "How?" The first, if not vain, is less than helpful, for most who are haunted by it ask it till it exhausts them. The better question to ask is "How?"

"The world breaks everyone," wrote Hemingway in *A Farewell to Arms*, "and afterward many are strong in the broken places." John Milton went blind and then wrote his greatest poetry. Beethoven lost his hearing and went on composing music anyway. Louis Pasteur was a paralytic at the age of forty-six. Nelson Mandela spent a lifetime on a prison island off Cape Town and became the first black president of the Republic of South Africa. Helen Keller suffered the unimaginable isolation of deafness and blindness but came to thank God for them both, believing that they had led her to her life's work. Dickens was able to go to school a total of four years of his life but became perhaps the greatest novelist in the English language. Dostoyevsky was sentenced to death, led to the gallows, pardoned just as the rope was to take his life, and exiled to Siberia. He returned to write greater novels than ever. Terry Waite, held hostage for years in Beirut, could say, "Christianity doesn't in any way lessen suffering. What it does is enable you to take it, to face it, to work through it and eventually to convert it."

I Know That God Is with Me

Among the comforts that soothe us when we suffer is the knowledge that others have passed through this place before and know it. In their shared experience, they are "with us." Planted at the center of the Christian faith is the cross. That cross is the sign that God has passed here before and is with us. God declares by this sign that "there is no pain that you can bear that I have not borne; there is no darkness that can overtake you that I have not seen; there is no fear that might grip you that I have not known. I have passed through it, and when you come to pass through it, I am with you."

Chapter 18

Stuff and Work

*T*he term "idolatry" is largely out of vogue, evoking as it does images of dour Old Testament prophets thundering against graven images. Yet two thoroughly modern idols sit enthroned at the center of our prosperous and hardworking society: consumerism and careerism. The venerable Christian answer to the question, "Who are you?" is "I am a child of God." Our faith stubbornly insists that human beings are defined in relationship to God and that the meaning and purpose of our lives are shaped in that relationship. So consumerism is idolatry when it suggests that the answer to the "Who are you?" question is "I am what I have." Careerism is idolatry when it answers the question with "I am what I do."

Stuff: Finding the Balance Point

Let me begin with two stories about money. A few years ago a friend told me about the high school reunion he had just attended. There were the usual tales about cheerleaders gone chubby and class nerds grown handsome. But his most poignant tale was about the guy who had won the lottery. In his prelottery days, this classmate had not been noticed much. He had come from a poor family, the son of a distant father and an alcoholic mother. He had gone to college but never finished. He had not married and had ended up with a job sorting mail.

A few years later, he won three million dollars in the New York State Lottery, a sum that would generate an annual income of a few hundred thousand dollars. Suddenly, every dream was within reach.

He quit his job and bought a big house on a couple of acres in a toney Long Island suburb. But soon, after a short-lived burst of popularity, he became vaguely suspicious of his friends and seldom went out, passing his days by fiddling around the house. He found himself with no abiding interests, indeed, no passion for anything. Depressed and lonely, he now complains that his income is simply not adequate.

The second story is about Frank McCourt's Pulitzer Prize–winning memoir, *Angela's Ashes,* a grueling account of the author's childhood in Ireland: hungry second-graders fighting for the apple peels left over from the teachers' lunches, babies starving, middle-aged men dying of tuberculosis, shoes repaired with old tires, four sick children sleeping in the same flea-ridden bed, no running water, no toilets—all on the banks of the River Shannon just fifty years ago.

I was flabbergasted to read a comment that the author made about the reaction to his book soon after it was published. McCourt said that in spite of page upon page of such horrific memories, some people had still managed to read the book as a romantic Irish memoir about growing up poor but happy in old Ireland. McCourt was mercilessly clear on this point. His impoverished childhood was not happy; it was irreducibly miserable. He left as soon as he could and emigrated to America.

These two stories are emblematic of our twin responses to the consumerism that defines our place and time. Ironically, we romanticize *both* wealth and poverty. We fantasize one moment about the rustic virtues of the unencumbered life, a simplicity free of the burdens and complications that come with owning stuff. The next moment we fantasize about what it would be like to be so rich we could move beyond the worries of never having enough. Both reactions are idolatrous because they ascribe to mere things a power over our lives that they do not have.

Once a rich young man knelt at Jesus' feet, addressed him flatteringly, and asked, "What must I do to inherit eternal life?" Jesus first answered by noting several of the Ten Commandments. The man responded that from his youth he had kept those laws. Then Jesus looked at him, loved him, and told him to liquidate his holdings, give the proceeds to the poor, and come follow him. The Gospel says that the young man was shocked at this answer and left sadly. It is one of the few instances in the Bible where someone says no to an invitation from Jesus—and it's because of money.

The passage has sometimes been taken as an injunction for Christians to live in literal poverty. Indeed, some early followers of Jesus did sell their goods and give what they had either to the poor or to a common purse. Later interpretations read the biblical call away from materialism as applicable to a special few, usually clergy and monastics. But few in our world have responded to this passage by a full retreat from the owning of things. We may own them with guilt, assuming that if we were "more spiritual" we would own less. We imagine that the choice before us is either elective poverty or yielding ourselves to the charms of the Shopping Channel, that it's either the monastery or the mall.

The deeper meaning of this story, however, and the truth about "stuff" in general, is revealed in Jesus' recognition that for this young man, wealth was an impediment to discipleship. Money, Jesus discerned, was his particular spiritual stumbling block as it is often the particular stumbling block of our consumer society. Jesus' call to him to leave his riches is not necessarily a call for all of us literally to do the same thing. Nevertheless, these words still make a demand, even if it is not the demand of poverty. They may or may not call us to poverty, but they clearly call us to surrender whatever it is in our lives that would be our "god" when it is not God.

So the story may not mean we have to sell our indulgences: the Buick and the summer cottage, the motorcycle or the camcorder. But it does mean that the position that these things occupy in our lives must be scrupulously examined. Do we strive for financial liquidity more than spiritual depth? Do we expend more passion on prosperity or prayer? Are our dreams most often dreams of things? Jesus' famous camel-through-the-eye-of-the-needle, an image imbedded in this story to describe how hard it is for the rich to get into heaven, is Jewish hyperbole at its most hyperbolic. Nevertheless, exaggerated or not, its disarmingly sharp point is that things can indeed block our way to God.

When we buy something new and open up the box, we are generally met with pages of printed material: owner's manuals, exploded assembly diagrams, directions for use, warranty cards, survey questionnaires. All these pages that come in the box fall into two categories: instructions and warnings. Instructions on assembly, use, and maintenance, and warnings not to let kids put pieces in their mouth, not to use this product in the bathtub, not to use this product without wearing safety goggles. Maybe they should put one more instruction page in every box. It could say, "Note: You are a fortunate consumer to have the ability to own this fine product. Remember to share what you have." And maybe they should put yet another warning label on every new product. Bold red letters on a white decal affixed to the side could read, "Warning: This thing, like all things, could be dangerous to your spiritual health."

But we must also remember that the same Jesus who told the rich young man to sell everything also spoke respectfully of material things, everything from rings to robes and pearls. The very doctrine of the incarnation of Christ, God in human form, implies an incarnation of the spiritual into the material. Incarnation is necessarily an affirmation of the potential goodness of the physical. The God we come to know in Scripture is the same Creator who fashioned this world of materiality and named it "good." Matter, after all, is one of God's best ideas. "God," quipped Robert Capon, gourmet cook and theologian, "is the biggest materialist there is. He invented the stuff." Not only did God invent it, God chose to enter into it. Jesus Christ, human and divine, stands as an embodied affirmation that God embraces base materiality; the merest stuff of this beautiful, ugly world is raised to heaven itself.

Christian faith is squared off against idolatrous consumerism today in much the same way it once fought another heresy named Gnosticism. Gnosticism was an ancient religious system that assumed life was essentially a showdown between the material and spiritual worlds. In this scheme, religion was about escaping the physical world for that of pure spirit. Gnostics, of course, found the incarnation scandalous because it integrated materiality and spirituality. Against these gnostics, orthodox Christianity defended the redeemability of the material and the beauty of the physical.

The very gratuitous loveliness of the material world and the superfluous variety and needless existence of so many delicate and awesome things seems testimony to the fact that their Creator would have us find joy in things, even ones that are not "practical." John Calvin wrote that for a person to find no joy in the beauty of things "apart from their necessary use . . . degrades him to a block."[1]

There is a delicate point of balance to be found between the denial of the material and the idolatry of consumerism; for most of us, it is located somewhere between the monastery and the mall. But the balance point is found not just in moderation. Moderation is generally a virtue, but most of us easily deceive ourselves about what is moderate.

In a scene in Tennessee Williams's play *Cat on a Hot Tin Roof*, Big Daddy and his son, Brick, are talking in the basement, surrounded by all the junk that Big Daddy has worked so hard for over the years. Brick is exploring questions of meaning far too sensitive for his father to understand. In the course of the conversation, he looks at all the stuff in the basement and asks a deeply theological question, "Big Daddy, why'd you buy all this junk?" "Because I wanted to live," he answers. "Because I wanted my life to amount to something."

Big Daddy's blindness was less to material moderation and more to the placing of things—money and houses, bank accounts and toys—precisely where they belong in our lives. And that place is where we do not expect them to fill the emptiness that aches for something more.

Work: Finding Another Balance Point

If consumerism is an idolatry that declares "I am what I have," careerism is idolatry that believes that "I am what I do." Christian faith has long affirmed the doctrine of vocation. At its broadest, vocation is simply the understanding that all men and women are called to meaningful work that directly or indirectly might bring benefit to others and even glory to God. Vocation is not just for ministers, but for all.

Vocation lies at that intersection where your joy and the needs of the world intersect. That is, meaningful work is work that is good for me and good for the world.

This is doubtless an intersection easier for a pediatrician to find than for the young woman working the drive-through window at McDonald's. Yet all things give God glory if you mean that they should. Even the ninety-year-old in the wheelchair in the nursing home hallway can offer her own work: the work of prayer, the work of a ready smile to the stressed attendant who is late wheeling her down to dinner. For many today, there may be several such successive vocational intersections in life. God has endowed each of us with particular talents. Our call is to use those abilities given us and the situations that providence has set before us in such a way that what we do day by day brings glory to God, benefit to others, and satisfaction to self.

But the goodness of work, like the goodness of things, becomes idolatrous the moment it jockeys itself to the center of our lives and settles into that place that can be filled by none save God. We live in a careerist world in which we ask strangers at parties, "What do you do?" by which we really mean "Who are you?" With some embarrassment, a friend once told me about his congregation's pictorial directory. Under each member's picture was his or her name, and under that was a notation of the person's job. The implication was that this was nothing less than a definition of the value of this person. However valuable our work may be, it is never who we are. Christian faith affirms the goodness of work in the doctrine of vocation. Again, the quest is to find that balance point between the idolatry of careerism on the one hand and work-as-a-grind on the other. The first part of the answer is moderation: a life balanced between work and play, career and family. But the second part of the answer is to resist the temptation to ask of our work what it cannot give. Work, like wealth, becomes an idol when we imagine that it is what saves us. It would have been truer if under the names and photos in my friend's church directory they had just put, "child of God."

Two radically dissimilar thinkers, both of whom we have met before in these pages, wrote about imagining themselves having died and gone to heaven. Both arrived with the books they had written, their life's work, to present at the pearly gates. Each imagined heaven's reaction to this presentation. But the celestial responses they envisioned could not have been more different, and their respective imaginings of the scene revealed the bottom-line truth about how each understood his work and himself.

Jean-Jacques Rousseau, the eighteenth-century Swiss-French secular philosopher and social theorist, had a profound effect in shaping not only the more disastrous chapters of the French Revolution but the modern Western mind itself. The second, Karl Barth, will be remembered by many as the greatest Christian theologian of the twentieth century. Also Swiss, he did most of his work in the years shadowed by the totalitarianisms of Hitler and Stalin. Barth laid out a rediscovery of the radically God-centered theology of Scripture and earlier Christian tradition.

In his last work, *Confessions*, Rousseau begins by imagining himself approaching the heavenly throne with his head held high (no bowing or praise, no fear or even awe). He carries a copy of his *Confessions*. All the company of heaven turn to face him, and they set aside their praise of God to listen to Rousseau's life story. The supposed brilliance and candor of his great work justifies him at the pearly gates.

Barth wrote far more pages than Rousseau and imagines himself arriving with his books not under his arm but in a pushcart. But, in Barth's imagining, the angels do not turn to him for a reading from his works. They laugh. Barth said, "I shall be able to dump even the *Church Dogmatics,* over the growth of which the angels have long been amazed, on some heavenly floor as a pile of waste paper."[2] Barth stands justified before God by neither his copious works nor his great sincerity but by the grace of God alone.

What fascinates me most about the contrast between these two great thinkers is their diametrically opposed understandings of the way in which their life's work mattered. Rousseau's view is in no sense proportional to anything transcendent, only to the work of other humans. He imagines that all heaven might well learn something from a few pages of *The Social Contract* or *Confessions*. He and his work stand at the center of the cosmos. In such a geography, Rousseau's life, thought, and work are themselves of ultimate importance. How understandable that the angels should cease from their praise of God and turn to hear the man read from his book.

Karl Barth knew that his theology mattered. He would have hardly poured his life into its endless pages if he had not held the highest estimation of the importance of his work. But his view of his life's work was proportional to God. Barth's passion for his work was in proportion to his understanding that in relationship to God, even the *Church Dogmatics* would end up "on some heavenly floor as a pile of waste paper."

This finely nuanced appreciation of the work of our lives, important but never ultimately so, is good news. It calls us to give ourselves passionately to working at those efforts that we are convinced make a difference. But it frees us from the crushing burden of imagining that it all depends on us and that what we do is our sole source of value as human beings. This is the very subtlety that poet T. S. Eliot gave voice to when he prayed, "Teach us to care and not to care." So we work, perhaps tirelessly. What we do day to day may matter immensely, but in the end it will save neither us nor the world.

Our world's idolatry of work is betrayed no more clearly than in the erosion of the ancient concept of Sabbath. The commandment "Remember the sabbath day, to keep it holy" was intended not only to balance work and nonwork, but to set work in relationship to God. Sabbath-keeping set aside a part of life for that which was deeper than what we do for a living. But as Sunday has become just another day, not only has time blurred into an unpunctuated continuum, but the sense of proportionality that Sabbath gave to workdays is gone. To keep Sabbath, at least by going to worship, is a bold declaration that who we are is not the same as what we do. Sixty minutes on a Sabbath morning directed toward God does more than give God an hour. It remembers that all time comes from God and is for God. Sabbath-keeping remembers that everything we work at, however valuable it may or may not be to us and to the world, exists in proportion to a God who values us not for what we do, but simply because we are.

Chapter 19

An Expansive Lifestyle

*T*he God encountered in Scripture and Christian tradition is a radically expansive deity. That is to say, this God is not self-contained. This God is no passionless block of mystery in distant space, no unfeeling ether diffuse in the cosmos. The God of the Bible is essentially and passionately relational: God reaches out in love by creating that which is not God, reaches out in love to a particular people in the Old Testament, and reaches out in love to all humanity in the incarnation of Jesus Christ. As we have seen in earlier chapters, this God of divine expansiveness is apprehended in the eloquent terms of Trinity. God the Father expands into *all* time and space as the Word that creates something out of nothing and then as the Word that dwells in Christ. And this God expands to *our* time and space as Holy Spirit, the Present Tense of God. The figure often used to picture Trinity is a simple equilateral triangle. This is no adequate picture of God, of course, but it can serve as an image of a God whose very being is relational.

The second image I would set before you is the cross, two lines—one vertical and the other horizontal. I often tell children that not only does the cross remind us of the length and breadth of God's love, but I invite them to imagine that each line reminds us of something more. The upright is like God's love come down to us, as it were, imagining for a moment that God is up and we are down. As such, the vertical is a drawing of the expansiveness of God. The crossbar, I then tell them, reminds us of the horizontal love we extend to others, indeed to the world, as we expand beyond self, just as God expands beyond God's Self. If I have attentive children on my hands, I might add that a cross is obviously not a cross if it has only one line. The expansiveness of Christian faith is both vertical and horizontal. "Jesus loves me" is only half the gospel without "Love your neighbor." And alone, "Love your neighbor" is a truncated gospel severed from its roots.

But the principal picture of expansiveness that I would sketch over this chapter is a circle growing out from the center of God. There is a three-step movement to this expansiveness. First, the expansive love of God inclines *me* toward a life of expansiveness. Second, in this life I reach beyond myself to love others and be in community with them. In such relationship I discover my full humanity. Third, these communities of relationship—family, friends, and church—are likewise impelled to live their corporate lives expansively, to forever expand their circle into the entire world. Just as I cannot know who I am without others, a community of faith discovers who it is only in living for more than itself.

The Bible is replete with stories of the risks implicit in this enlarging of the circle. In the Old Testament, God tells Jonah to travel to notorious Nineveh, a dissolute and pagan city hated by pious Israelites. There he was to preach repentance so the Ninevites might be spared. But saving Ninevites from perdition is the last thing Jonah has in mind; indeed, he cannot fathom that even God should love them. Jonah heads in the opposite direction and meets with both shipwreck and the famous fish. But eventually Jonah sulks his way to Nineveh, preaches repentance halfheartedly, and then mopes when the Ninevites actually repent and are spared. The force of the story is the expansive circle of God's love and, by implication, our love, even to Nineveh, beyond the compass of human moral imagination.

In the New Testament, Jesus' conflicts with religious authorities, most often scribes and Pharisees, are usually over the question of the limits of God's love. Jesus is roundly criticized for associating with those popularly imagined to be outside any conceivable circle of grace: questionable women, tax collectors, Gentiles, and sinners in general. Time and again, the presenting problem is whom Jesus eats with, talks to, or loves.

After the Gospels, the book of Acts tells the story of the expansion of the church in the days after Easter. In no time, Jesus' followers run and tell everybody the too-good-to-be-true news of God's triumph over death. Like circular wavelets emanating in widening rings after a stone is thrown into a quiet pond, the gospel expands outward. At first it was the women disciples who had gone to the tomb, then the men among them. Next the news is spoken to others beyond the circle, and suddenly the Easter expansion gets edgy. The disciples begin telling *everybody* the story, and in no time the "wrong" people are being pulled into the circle.

At first it was Samaritans, those racially mixed, theologically deviant, superstitious, embarrassing half cousins to the Jews. Next it was foreigners, those untouchable Gentiles. The disciple Philip met an Ethiopian, a Gentile and a eunuch to boot—ritually impure on two counts and ineligible to even enter the Temple. But Philip preached the gospel to this strange foreigner, who was baptized and suddenly no longer one of "them" but one of "us." First it was heretics, now it's foreigners, and finally the enemy himself is pulled into the circle: Saul, arch-Pharisee, who had held the coats of those who murdered the Christian martyr Stephen, was en route to Damascus to arrest Christians. He suddenly found himself blinded on the road, stunned by an inexplicable experience of the living Christ. He became Paul, "one of us," and the circle has expanded beyond conceiving.

In the preface to his book *The Intrusive Word*, William Willimon, now a bishop in Alabama, tells this story about one of the churches he had served earlier in his career, a small congregation that decided they needed to add new members:

> We organized ourselves into groups of two and, on the appointed Sunday afternoon, we set out to visit, to invite people to our church. . . . Each team was given a map with their assigned street.
>
> Helen and Gladys were given a map. They were clearly told to go down Summit Drive and to *turn right*. That's what they were told. I heard the team leader tell them, "You go to Summit Drive and turn right. Do you hear me, Helen, that's down Summit Drive and turn right?"
>
> But Helen and Gladys, both approaching eighty, after a lifetime of teaching elementary school, were better at giving than receiving directions. They turned left, . . . into the housing projects west of Summit. Which meant that Helen and Gladys proceeded to evangelize the "wrong" neighborhood. . . .

Willimon says that later that afternoon, the teams returned to the church to give their report. Helen and Gladys had only one interested person, a woman named Verleen.

> The next Sunday, Helen and Gladys proudly presented Verleen at the eleven o'clock service. . . . Verleen liked the service so much that she wanted to attend the Women's Thursday Morning Bible Study. . . . Verleen appeared, proudly clutching her new Bible, a gift of Helen's circle, the first Bible she had ever seen.

Willimon continues his tale that next Thursday at a Bible study focusing on temptation: "'Have any of you ever been faced with temptation and, with Jesus' help, resisted?'" After one class member told a tale about being tempted to keep a loaf of bread that she had not been charged for at the supermarket, Verleen spoke:

> "A couple of years ago, I was into cocaine real big. . . . You know how that stuff makes you crazy. Well, anyway, my boyfriend, not the one I've got now . . . we knocked over a gas station one night—got two hundred dollars out of it. . . . Well, my boyfriend, he says to me, 'Let's knock over the Seven-Eleven down on the corner.' And something says to me, 'No, I've held up that gas station with you, but I ain't going to hold up no convenience store.' He beat . . . me, but I still said No. It felt great to say No. . . . Made me feel like somebody."

After a moment of stunned silence, Willimon manages to mutter:

> "Well, er, uh, that's resisting temptation." . . . After I stumbled out of the church parlor and was standing in the church parking lot, helping Helen into her Plymouth, she said to me, "You know, I can't wait to get home and get on the phone and invite people to next Thursday. Your Bible studies used to be dull. I think we could get a crowd for this!"

Then Willimon concludes with these words:

> Time and again in our life together, just when we get everything figured out, the pews all bolted down, and everyone blissfully adjusted to the status quo, God has intruded, inserting some topsy-turvy-turned life like Verleen just to remind the baptized that God is large, unmanageable, and full of surprises.[1]

The expansiveness of the church is the macroexpression of the individual believer's expansion beyond self. Both are inspired by and analogical to the fundamentally expansive love of God, a passion that refuses to acknowledge boundaries. The expansive love of the church is traditionally divided between evangelism and mission. Evangelism is the church's expression of the love of God in word. Mission is the church's expression of the love of God in deed. There is a standing debate between Christians who believe that the gospel is mostly about proclaiming the word that changes individual lives and those who believe it's more about doing deeds that can make the world a better place. But in truth, the church is called to love expansively in both ways. Neither word nor deed has integrity without the other. Arie Brouwer, who led the National Council of Churches through the 1980s, put it succinctly: "Spirituality and solidarity are inseparable. I question a spirituality that doesn't engage itself in the issues of the time. I question also a solidarity that is divorced from spirituality, because it soon slips into activism and burnout."

If Christians live expansively in the larger world, whether individually or corporately in church, they will inevitably collide with politics. That word has grown almost pejorative in recent years, implying the compromise of one's ideals, if not the outright corruption of all who touch the political. But politics are as inevitable to living groups of people as breathing is to living individuals. All communities—families and churches, small towns and nations—need to hammer out decisions about their life together. All associations of individuals—familial, civil, and religious—need structures for leadership. They plot their courses in the tumble of discourse and compromise. Alliances of the like-minded form to further common goals. This political process is only as noble or sorry as the individuals involved in it.

People of faith, if they care about more than self, will inevitably find themselves somewhere in this process. An expansive love for the world makes the interaction unavoidable. Because our values are shaped by our faith, it is not just only natural but necessary that those sacred values help shape secular convictions. However, the temptation that believers often face and occasionally fall for is to entirely identify some particular political philosophy with the faith itself. Not only does such a misstep usually end up a political and theological disaster, it is finally idolatrous. God's will cannot be subsumed in any particular party or any social philosophy. God is beyond the human categories of Republican or Democrat, socialist or free-market, left or right. Our faith shapes the values that we bring into the world of the political, but none of the human categories of that world are the same thing as the will of God.

Life's journey moves through the very world that God loves so much that God would send the Son into it, enfleshed in its very materiality. We move through it both estranged from it and loving it tirelessly. As individuals, we are not self-contained and isolated spots on the map; rather, we live expansively in widening circles of relationship. Communities of faith that bind individuals together in relationship also must live expansively, reaching beyond their respective circles to love the world that God loves. Such an expanding geography is an earthly imitation of heaven. It would reflect in time the very life of the God of eternity, whose very nature is expansive.

In the mid-1980s, a year or two after the last Arab-Israeli war, I met a man named Fuad Bahnan, an Arab born in Jerusalem. Recently deceased, he was a minister in the Evangelical Synod of Syria and Lebanon. For over thirty years, Mr. Bahnan served a small congregation in Beirut. When I met him, he was still serving this congregation in overwhelmingly Muslim West Beirut. In 1983 the armies of Israel drove north into Lebanon. No one knew how far north they would go. Few people in Lebanon thought that they would go as far as Beirut. But members of Bahnan's church thought that the Israelis would indeed take Beirut and would then attempt to starve out any Palestinian fighters left in the city. So the session of Bahnan's church decided to arrange for the purchase of a vast amount of canned food for the siege.

They were right, of course. The siege came. West Beirut was totally cut off. No one could enter or leave. No food was allowed in. The session of Pastor Bahnan's church met again, this time to make arrangements for distributing the food they had stockpiled. At that session meeting, two different proposals came to the table. The first went like this: The food would be distributed first to members of the congregation, then as supplies permitted, to other Christians in West Beirut, and last, if any was left over, to the Muslims. The second proposal on the table was quite different. This motion was that the food be distributed first to Muslim neighbors, then to nonmember Christians, and last, if there was any left over, to members of the church.

The session meeting lasted six hours. It ended when an older, quiet, and much-respected elder—a woman—stood up, and cried out: "If we do not demonstrate the love of Christ in this place, who will?" The second proposal was passed. The food was distributed first to Muslims, then to other Christians, and finally, to members of the congregation. In the end, there was enough for everyone.

Chapter 20

All or Nothing

I once had a friend named Tom, an engineer with a philosophical bent. We used to ride motorcycles together on Saturday mornings. We'd always have coffee first and talk about bikes and life. He always talked about both in an engineer sort of way. I remember him once drawing a graph-like picture of life. Birth was on the left side, and the end of the journey was at the right of the graph. Your years unfolded from left to right across the sheet. There was not much new to this; the genius was in its up-and-down dimension. Stacked atop one another in his life graph were colored bands of varying height. These bands represented what occupied your life at any point in the trip from left to right. Tom called these "bands of interest." For instance, for the first twenty-some years of your life, the yellow education band would probably be very thick. Then after you finished school, that band would grow narrower—not that you weren't still learning, just that education became a smaller part of your life. Then should you choose to marry, a new band representing your own family would enter the diagram. If children came along, that family band would widen as that piece of your life got more and more important. There might be a band for your hobbies—motorcycles, painting pictures, or golf. There would be a band called "friendships," and for many people a very broad band called "career." For some people, Tom observed, there would also be a band of interest called "religious faith."

This, of course, is a precise image of how so many people misunderstand the spiritual life. They imagine that spirituality is one band of interest in life. God is a priority among any number of life's priorities. At first, it appears to be a sensibly proportioned life, a well-balanced stew, you might say: a cup of career, a cup of play, a cup of family or friends, and finally, a cup of God.

My friend Tom was a committed Christian. And he was a savvy enough Christian to understand that identifying religion as just one of a number of bands of interest on your life's chart just wouldn't have cut it with Jesus. If there is one bottom-line truth that Jesus is insistent about, it is that if you should choose to follow him, you have to follow him with all of you, not just a part of you. This radical demand is captured in an awkward and thoroughly unmodern word that Scripture uses to talk about the journey of faith. In English, the word is translated as "repent." The first thing Jesus says in Mark's Gospel, probably the oldest of the four, is "Repent, and believe in the gospel" (1:15). Most people think "repent" means to "get on your knees and blurt out your sins." But this is a misreading of the Greek word behind it. *Metanoia* literally means "to turn around." It means "to do a 180." If you're going east and do a *metanoia*, now you're going west. If you're going south and do a *metanoia*, now you're going north. The point is that if you "repent, and believe in the gospel," not only are you not just listing your sins, you're not doing a mere ten-degree course correction either. The implication of *metanoia* is that Christ demands nothing less than a 180-degree turn. That is, God asks for everything. Everything we are is to be turned around toward God at the center. If we occupy the center, God cannot, so everything in us that demands to be perched on the throne must slide off and move toward the circumference of a God-centered circle. Faith cannot be one band of interest in a life blithely marching along in the same old direction. If faith means anything, it is nothing less than a 180-degree reorientation of the whole self toward God.

That ancient pagan tribe of lusty warriors named the Franks were among the first of the Germans to be converted to Christianity. Like many of the tribes during this era, the Franks were converted to Jesus en masse, and the group underwent baptism by wading into a river to be baptized by the thousands. They understood what this meant at some level, namely, that this would make them followers of a new king, Jesus. They perhaps understood that this Jesus was called a "Prince of Peace," doubtless an odd title to their ears. The story is told that when these Frankish warriors came to be baptized in the water of the Rhine or the Rhone, they were always careful to hold their swords above their heads out of the waters of baptism, not to save them from rust but to keep them from Jesus.

It wouldn't do then; it won't do now. This Jesus asks for everything. You can't hold your sword out of the water. You can't hold your career out of the water. You can't hold your idle pastimes out of the water. You can't hold your checkbook out of the water. You can't even hold your love life out of the water. Everything has to go under so that it can rise again. Nothing can be held back. Faith in God cannot be just another "band of interest." On this journey across life's graph paper, any God worth the name can never be confined to a light blue strip called religion, however broad it might be.

Let me carry Tom's graph image one more step. Our lives do indeed have bands of interest: work and family, hobbies and school. But faith is not one of these particular bands. Rather, faith is a cross-hatching that begins to overlay all of the colored bands of your life when first God enters into the movement across the graph. The cross-hatching of faith is laid over the red band of work, over the green of family, over the beige of volunteer work, and over the pink of Saturday pastimes, not necessarily crowding any of it out, but transforming it all into what it was created to be in the first place.

So work is part of life—but not just for the buck or the prestige or even the personal satisfaction; rather, work also comes to be for the good of others, even the glory of God. School is part of life—but not just education to get me ahead; rather, education is for the good of the world. Marriage and family and friendships may be part of life—but not just to please me or to keep me company on quiet nights; rather, these relationships are made of such love that they come to light up the dimness of the world. Perhaps the sharpest edge of the Christian gospel is this radical demand for all. Only in this great yielding of all can all that I give come back transformed. So I let go of my anxious grip. I yield to the God in whom and through whom and with whom the journey moves across the page. And then this day-after-day movement is transformed into the pilgrimage of high joy and deep purpose that it was intended to be from the very beginning.

Afterword

*I*magine God standing on your front porch. . . .
God knocks at my door. . . . "Rent is cheap," I say.
"I don't want to rent. I want to buy," says God. . . .
"I might let you have a room or two."
"Thanks," says God. "I like what I see."
"I'd like to give you the whole house, but I'm not sure—"
"Think on it," says God. "I wouldn't put you out. . . . You'd have
   more space than you've ever had."
"I don't understand. . . ."
"I know," says God, "but I can't tell you about that. You'll have
   to discover it for yourself. That can happen only if you let me
   have the whole house."
"A bit risky," I say.
"Yes," says God, "but try me. . . ."

(Edited from a longer unpublished
poem by Margaret Halaska)

Notes

CHAPTER 1

1. E. F. Schumacher, *A Guide for the Perplexed* (New York: Harper & Row, 1977), 1–2.

CHAPTER 2

1. As quoted in Patrick Henry, *The Ironic Christian's Companion* (New York: Riverhead, 1999), 17–19.

2. As quoted in Nicky Gumbel, *Questions of Life* (Colorado Springs: David C. Cook, 1996), 13–14.

3. Howard Mouma, "Conversations with Camus," *Christian Century* 117, no. 18 (June 7–14, 2000): 644–45.

CHAPTER 3

1. C. S. Lewis, *Surprised by Joy* (New York: Harcourt, Brace & World, 1955), 227.

2. From Francis Thompson, "The Hound of Heaven," as quoted in *Chapters into Verse,* ed. Robert Atwan and Laurance Wieder (New York: Oxford University Press, 2000), 364.

3. Victor Hugo, *Les Misérables* (New York: Fawcett Premier, 1961), 32.

CHAPTER 4

1. Fyodor Dostoyevsky, "The Grand Inquisitor," as quoted in *Man and God*, ed. Victor Gollancz (New York: Houghton Mifflin, 1951), 174–75.

CHAPTER 5

1. Donald W. McCullough, *The Trivialization of God* (Colorado Springs: Navpress, 1995), 33–34.

2. Ben Patterson, *The Grand Essentials* (Waco, TX: Word, 1987), 146, quoted in McCullough, *Trivialization of God,* 33–34.

3. Eberhard Busch, *Karl Barth,* trans. John Bowden (Philadelphia: Fortress Press, 1976), 489, quoted in McCullough, *Trivialization of God,* 33–34.

4. As quoted in William H. Willimon, "Formed by the Saints," *Christian Century* 113, no. 5 (Feb. 7–14, 1996): 137.

5. Albert Schweitzer, *Out of My Life and Thought* (New York: Henry Holt, 1933), 71–72. Schweitzer had ended his classic, *The Quest of the Historical Jesus,* with these words.

CHAPTER 6

1. William H. Willimon, "Letting Go Down Here," *Christian Century* 103, no. 8 (March 5, 1986): 232.

CHAPTER 7

1. Quoted in Robert Johnson, *The Meaning of Christ* (Philadelphia: Westminster Press, 1958), 10.

2. Robert N. Bellah, *Habits of the Heart* (New York: Harper & Row, 1985), 221.

3. C. S. Lewis, *Mere Christianity* (New York: Macmillan, 1952), 57.

4. I am deeply indebted to Leanne Van Dyk's lucid presentation of Anselm and Abelard's theology in her superb book *Believing in Jesus Christ,* Foundations of Christian Faith (Louisville, KY: Geneva Press, 2002).

5. Peter Abelard, "Exposition of the Epistle to the Romans," in *A Scholastic Miscellany: Anselm to Ockham,* ed. Eugene R. Fairweather (Philadelphia: Westminster Press, 1981), 283.

CHAPTER 9

1. Francis Thompson, "In No Strange Land," in *The New Oxford Book of Christian Verse,* ed. Donald Davie (Oxford: Oxford University Press, 1981), 256–57.

2. Belden Lane, "The Ordinary as Mask of the Holy," *Christian Century* 101, no. 29 (Oct. 3, 1984): 899.

CHAPTER 11

1. Donald W. McCullough, *The Trivialization of God* (Colorado Springs: Navpress, 1995), 13.

2. Annie Dillard, *Teaching a Stone to Talk* (New York: Harper & Row, 1982), 40–41.

CHAPTER 12

1. Archbishop Iakovos, *Faith for a Lifetime* (New York: Doubleday, 1988).

CHAPTER 14

1. Taken from an unpublished lecture by Andrew Purves.

2. Ibid.

CHAPTER 17

1. William Sloane Coffin, "Alex's Death" (sermon, Riverside Church, New York City, January 23, 1983).

2. Thomas Merton, *The Seven Storey Mountain* (New York: Harcourt, Brace, 1948), 111.

3. Kathleen Norris, *Amazing Grace* (New York: Riverhead, 1998), 13.

CHAPTER 18

1. John Calvin, *Institutes of the Christian Religion* 3.10.3; ed. John T. McNeill, trans. Ford Lewis Battles, LCC (Philadelphia: Westminster Press, 1960).

2. Eberhard Busch, *Karl Barth,* trans. John Bowden (Philadelphia: Fortress Press, 1976), 489.

CHAPTER 19

1. William H. Willimon, *The Intrusive Word* (Grand Rapids: Eerdmans, 1994), 1–4.

Other Books by Michael Lindvall

The Good News from North Haven

Leaving North Haven

What Did Jesus Do? A Crash Course on the Life of Jesus